Toward Speaking Excellence

The MICHIGAN Guide to Maximizing Your Performance on the TSE® Test and Other Speaking Tests

SECOND EDITION

DEAN PAPAJOHN

Ann Arbor
University of Michigan Press

*TSE is a registered trademark of Educational Testing Service.
This publication is not endorsed or approved by ETS.

Acknowledgments

This second edition has been improved by the contributions of a number of people. My sincere thanks to: the students who piloted practice materials, many of whose responses are included in these pages; Laura Hahn, Barbara Schroeder, Diana Steele, Patti Watts, and Damon DellaFave, who offered suggestions and feedback on drafts of various sections; Wayne Wilson for the vivid graphic arts accompanying the narrate a story questions; Kelly Sippell and the University of Michigan Press team for their professional advice and assistance with the publication process; and Bethany, Sarah, and Danny for their loving support.

Contents

A Note to Instructors Regarding
This Book and Test Preparation

This book is intended to encourage learners to practice speaking English and analyze their own speaking with a critical ear. While learners may use this book as a self-study tool, it is not intended to replace ESL classes; this book is designed as a tool for both learners and ESL instructors. While the material is directed toward the TSE® Test and SPEAK® Test, the communication strategies shared here should be useful for learners preparing for other types of oral exams, interviews, and performance tests as well. Practice over time will help learners develop skills to be able to respond appropriately to a variety of situations. Learners should practice responding to a variety of tasks, not just those in this book. If learners spend more time speaking English because of this book and think about what and how they communicate more than they have in the past, then this book's purpose will be achieved.

Test preparation has often been misunderstood. Can students benefit from test preparation? Does test preparation falsely inflate skill levels? Should ESL instructors dissuade learners from any type of test preparation? Four common misconceptions in preparing for oral tests that I discussed in *TESOL Matters* (Oct/Nov 2000, vol. 10, no. 4) are summarized here.

- **Misconception 1: Test preparation focuses on tricks, not skills, and therefore inflates scores.**

   Some test preparation may indeed lack substance, but solid communication strategies can be taught and are useful for responding to tests, and more important, for real-life communication. Communication strategies can include organized responses, organizational markers, audience awareness, and the importance of stress and tone. Inflated scores occur when examinees score better than would be reflected in their actual skills. If test questions and the scoring rubric of a test accurately focus on important aspects of communication, there is no reason to think that an examinee will sound organized, cohesive, and fluent on a test, but not in other real-life settings. Improving communication skills so that learners improve their scores is an appropriate goal for test preparation.

- **Misconception 2: Test preparation destroys spontaneous speech.**

  Spontaneity refers to responding based on a natural feeling from within. Native speakers have access to conscious and subconscious templates for a variety of communication, from letters and memos to introductions and speeches. Knowledge of these templates should not be assumed to exist for a person communicating in a second language and culture. However, there is no reason to keep these templates hidden from nonnative speakers. Communicative strategies and spontaneity are not mutually exclusive. When communication strategies are learned well, they can be applied spontaneously, in a way similar to native speakers. While memorized answers interfere with testing, knowledge of cultural and linguistic conventions aids communication and should be a part of learning and testing.

- **Misconception 3: Teaching specific organizational markers limits the range of responses.**

  Exposing students to specific organizational markers and how they are used in context does not limit them to those words and phrases studied. The goal is to broaden learners' understanding of the importance of organizational markers in such a way that they will recognize them more frequently and will apply them appropriately. Memorizing words and inserting them without proper understanding will not make communication sound more fluent, whether on a test or in another communication context.

- **Misconception 4: Structured language samples are not as effective as impromptu language samples for learning oral communication.**

  Structured language is more common in written form, so some may argue against its use in teaching oral skills. However, impromptu speech is filled with incomplete sentences, hesitations, and informal structure. Therefore, impromptu speech can sometimes prove frustrating and confusing to learners. If the ultimate goal is clear communication rather than imitation of native speakers, structured language can be an effective teaching tool. In this book, model responses, authentic responses, and modified authentic responses have been used.

These and other misconceptions about test preparation continue to circulate for a couple of reasons. The first reason is the existence of test preparation that is poorly conceived and that aims to improve scores without improving skills. This is usually associated with cramming. Cramming does not involve long-term learning, nor does it encourage extrapolating learning to new contexts. The second reason is based on the instruments used in oral assessment. Common complaints about oral testing are: the lack of interactivity (especially in semi-direct recorded exams); the fact that scoring rubrics may not account for certain qualities (such as spontaneity or nuanced responses); the generalizability of certain language functions (such as complaining and apologizing); and the level of skill needed to score well (based on score levels and cut-off scores). While the ESL profession works toward improving testing instruments, we can harness the motivation that test preparation offers to help students learn sound communication strategies.

A Note to Learners

In addition to communication strategies, this book contains many sample responses to all the question types on the TSE® Test. These are not intended to be followed as a script, but to highlight what makes communication effective in various situations. You are encouraged to record your own responses and listen to and analyze yourself. You may find it helpful to work with a friend or colleague who is also interested in improving his or her English communication skills. Ideally, you will have an experienced ESL instructor who can give you feedback as well. When you record yourself, don't try to sound like someone else. Develop your own communication style. Practice the strategies you learn from this book, and draw on your own personality and strengths to become an effective communicator. Language is a tool for you to use, and it is my desire that this book will help you gain confidence and mastery of that tool in all of your communications.

— PART 1 —

Introduction to
Oral Proficiency Testing

–1–

Preparing for the TSE® Test and Other Speaking Tests

> In this chapter you will:
>
> - Consider what makes communication effective.
> - Learn how this book is organized.
> - Learn the four competencies that define communicative competence for the TSE® test.
> - Learn general TSE® test-preparation strategies.

What Makes Communication Effective?

As we begin, consider a situation where you had trouble communicating with someone else in English. Describe your experience, including where you were, who you were speaking with, what you were talking about, and why you think you had trouble communicating.

_____

_____

_____

_____

_____

_____

Now review your incident alone or with a partner and identify communication skills you could have employed to better get your meaning across.

_____

_____

_____

_____

_____

_____

Even native speakers of English run into miscommunications, so having strategies to overcome these inevitable communication problems is important. An effective communicator has a storehouse of strategies to communicate different things in different ways, as the situation calls for. Throughout this book you will learn how to effectively communicate in many situations you will face in real life and on the TSE® Test or SPEAK® Test. Language learning strategies and communication strategies will be marked throughout the book with this symbol ●➔.

How This Book Is Organized

The new TSE® test consists of three warm-up questions and nine rated questions. This book will take you through a practice test question by question. The sample questions used in this book are similar to those published by ETS (ETS 2003) in their 2003–04 *TSE Bulletin* and on the ETS website. ETS released these questions to show examinees samples of typical TSE® questions so examinees could "become familiar with the TSE" before actually taking the test. Information on how to register for the TSE® is provided in Chapter 15.

In Chapter 2 the TSE® score levels and scoring criteria are explained, and sample responses at different score levels are presented and discussed. Chapter 3 provides an overview of pronunciation. Clear pronunciation is essential for responding to all TSE® questions and for effective communication in general. A sample test is presented in Chapter 4 to introduce the test format and typical questions. Each type of TSE® Test question is discussed in detail in Chapters 5–14. You will see sample test questions shown in **bold lettering** surrounded by a single-lined box. The time allotted for the response is given in seconds inside the parentheses following the question. Sample questions look like this:

> **Sample question.** (60 seconds)

A sample answer in _**bold, italic lettering**_ in a double-lined box follows each question. Sample answers look like this:

> _**Sample answer.**_

In this second edition of *Toward Speaking Excellence,* actual student responses have been used or modified to highlight specific characteristics of effective communication. Actual responses may include disfluencies like excessive pausing or filler sounds, yet it is hoped that the realistic speech samples will lead to solid communication advice. We have tried to make the text match, as closely as possible, the spoken response. Language is complex so not all errors or all strengths of each response will be discussed. Rather, particular communication features will be emphasized to help cover a variety of skills and concepts for effective communication. Practice exercises are intended to help you focus on specific communication skills and strategies and are marked throughout the book with this symbol 🔊. In addition to the practice exercises, practice questions at the end of Chapters 5–14 provide you with the opportunity to apply the oral language skills discussed throughout this book. Chapter 15 provides practical test-taking tips for before, during, and after the TSE®. Chapter 16 contains two complete sample TSE-like tests for further practice. (These questions are not actual TSE® questions.)

Since some institutions may still be using the Retired TSE® or SPEAK®

Test, Chapters 17–20 provide background for the types of questions that are found on that test.

Four Rating Criteria

Raters of the TSE® Test focus on four areas of communicative competence. These areas are language function, appropriateness, coherence/cohesion, and accuracy.

- **Language functions** *include narrating, comparing, giving and defending an opinion, responding to a hypothetical situation, describing and analyzing a graph, extending a greeting, responding to a phone message, giving a progress report, etc.*

  Each question focuses on one or more language functions. While you may include other language functions in your response, the focus of your response should address the language functions stated in the question.

- **Appropriateness** *refers to responding with language appropriate for the intended audience or situation.*

  In some questions you are asked to respond to the narrator without any specifics given. In this situation, respond with a polite, friendly tone, as if you were talking with a respected colleague. Other questions may ask you to imagine you are talking to a friend, supervisor, business associate, customer, classmate, professor, medical professional, or patient. Sometimes the test specifies that you are talking with someone who works at the same company or institution as you. At other times you are asked to pretend to talk to someone without background on the topic you are addressing. Use language appropriate for whatever situation and audience that are specified.

- **Coherence/Cohesion** *reflects the ways language is organized (coherence) and how ideas relate to each other (cohesion).*

  It is important that your responses are not ambiguous. Opinions and recommendations should be stated clearly. Supporting reasons should clearly connect to the main idea. Steps in a process or events in a story should be ordered logically, described clearly, and connect smoothly. Be specific enough in your responses so that listeners do not have to interpret or supplement what you are saying in order to understand your meaning.

- **Accuracy** *includes pronunciation, grammar, fluency, and vocabulary.*
  Although there are a number of dialects of English, the standard for the TSE® and SPEAK® is the English of a university-educated person in the United States.

Sometimes when a speaker focuses on vocabulary or grammar or pronunciation, fluency suffers. Focused practice on oral English over a long period of time will help develop fluency with accurate vocabulary, grammar, and pronunciation. Tips on how to excel in each of these four areas are provided throughout this book. It is helpful to obtain feedback on your communication ability from knowledgeable ESL instructors. It is also important to develop skills to analyze your own speaking ability.

General Test-Preparation Strategies

In order to maximize your performance on the TSE® Test, you can prepare in the following ways.

1. Become familiar with the standard directions for the test.
2. Become familiar with typical sample questions for the test.
3. Become familiar with the rating criteria of *language functions, appropriateness, coherence/cohesion,* and *accuracy* and how they relate to good answers for test questions.
4. Practice answering sample questions on your own and in the specific time allotted.

When you take the TSE®, the questions are not only given orally, but the full questions are generally shown printed in the test book. As the question is being given orally, you should follow along in the test book. Listen carefully to the question because you may get clues on how to pronounce certain words or phrases that will be useful to you in your answer. Make sure you understand exactly what the question is asking. If your answer does not match the question asked, you may not succeed in the language function or appropriateness of response. The last two questions have oral components to the questions that are not written in the test booklet. You may find it helpful to jot down key words or phrases related to the listening portion so you can easily recall the main points. Pencil and paper are available in the new TSE® Test. However, pencil and paper are generally not allowed in the SPEAK® Test.

It is best to concentrate on one question at a time. Try not to focus on the clock. If you complete the practice exercises in this book you should have a good idea in your mind of how long you have to respond to each type of question. It is more important to focus on speaking than to focus on time remaining. When the response time is completed for a particular question, you will hear the test narrator say the number of the next test question, or begin directions for a new section of the test. If by chance you do poorly on one question, do not let it hinder the remainder of your performance. Instead, put that question behind you and concentrate on the question at hand. If you do not finish your response but are clearly on task and accomplishing the language function appropriately, coherently, and accurately, then your score will not be penalized for not finishing the task. However, responses that are incomplete due to disfluencies, such as lack of organization or lack of vocabulary, will not be given maximum scores.

Some speakers believe they will sound more fluent if they memorize some standard phrases, such as *historically speaking* or *such and such is a controversial issue.* In most cases these memorized phrases sound forced and unnatural and should be avoided. For example, if you are asked to give your opinion, it may sound too formal to start out by referring to history or saying the issue is controversial. Studying sample responses can help you see what makes effective and ineffective communication, but samples should not be memorized and forced into other contexts. Practice creating your own language when answering questions. Listen to your answers, think about ways to improve your response, and answer again. With practice you should be able to respond in your own words to any question.

As much as you can, put the testing environment out of your mind. If your test is given in a language laboratory with a lot of other people, be prepared to hear a buzz of noise when everyone is responding. Always take a few seconds to think about your answer before responding, even if other people jump right into responding. Likewise, if you finish a few seconds before the allotted time is up, don't worry if other people are still speaking. To help you put the testing environment out of your mind, try to answer the questions as if you were talking to someone in person and really desired to communicate that specific information. If you are thinking in the back of your mind how dreadful it is to be taking this test, it is liable to show up negatively in the way you respond. On the other hand, if you put enthusiasm into your voice, your intonation will reflect it and you will be seeking ways to effectively communicate your thoughts. Remember, the actual TSE® Test time is only about 20 minutes, so it is important to maximize your speaking performance during that time. The sample questions and answers that follow will help you to do your best when you take the TSE® Test.

–2–

Test Scoring

In this chapter you will:

- Learn about the scoring scale used for the TSE® Test.
- Learn how the scoring scale relates to the four communicative competencies.
- See example responses at various score levels and learn why they were scored at that particular level.

Scoring Scale

The TSE® scores range from 20 to 60 in five-point increments. So possible scores include 20, 25, 30, 35, 40, 45, 50, 55, and 60. You should not worry that you have to speak like a native speaker of English to receive a score of 60. Since the TSE® was designed for nonnative speakers of English, a native speaker of English would be expected to score well beyond a 60 if higher scores could be given (ETS 1996). Therefore, a high score on the TSE® is not out of reach of a nonnative speaker of English.

There is no universal passing score for the TSE®. Different institutions, whether they are universities or licensing boards, are responsible for setting their own cut-off scores (ETS 1996), so you should check with your institution to find out the minimum score you need. If you take the TSE®, ETS will rate your responses and report your scores to you and to the institutions you indicated on the mailing instruction form. If you take the SPEAK® Test, the institution that gave you the test will rate your responses and report your score. Institutions administering the SPEAK® use ETS's guidelines (ETS 1996) for scoring; this local training of raters and local rating of tests may produce some slight variability in rating between institutions and ETS (Sarwark 1995). For that reason, institutions do not generally report SPEAK® scores to other institutions, whereas ETS will report TSE® scores to all institutions.

Communicative Competencies and Scoring

Each of the even-numbered score levels have general descriptions that relate to communication ability and performance of task. Furthermore, these score levels have descriptors that relate to each of the four communication competencies. A summary of the rating scale is shown.

60 Almost always adequate communication and performance of task

>   Language functions addressed
>   Language appropriate for the audience
>   Language coherent and cohesive
>   Language linguistically accurate

50 Generally adequate communication and performance of task

>   Language functions generally addressed
>   Language generally appropriate for the audience
>   Language generally coherent and cohesive
>   Language generally linguistically accurate

40 Somewhat adequate communication and performance of task

>   Language functions somewhat addressed
>   Language somewhat appropriate for the audience
>   Language somewhat coherent and cohesive
>   Language somewhat linguistically accurate

30 Generally not adequate communication and performance of task

>   Language functions generally not addressed
>   Language generally not appropriate for the audience
>   Language generally incoherent and noncohesive
>   Language with generally poor linguistic accuracy

> **20 Not adequate communication and performance of task**
>
> Language functions not addressed
> Language not appropriate for the audience
> Language not coherent and not cohesive
> Language with poor linguistic accuracy

Here is another way to describe what these scores mean. Sixty means you are always understood by the rater and that the rater does not have to apply extra effort in understanding you. Fifty means that you are generally understandable, even though there are errors. Both 50 and 60 are positive scores in that communication has been successful. Forty is the middle-of-the-road score, sometimes positive, sometimes negative. At times a 40 is understandable, but at other times the rater has difficulty understanding what was said. That is, the rater must apply effort to understand a 40. Thirty means that although the examinee has responded, not much of what was said addresses the task or makes sense. Twenty means the rater doesn't really understand what the examinee is trying to communicate. Both 20 and 30 are negative scores where ideas are not communicated clearly.

It is interesting to note that the speaker's ability to communicate is rated in part on the listener's ability to understand. Someone who knows you well, like a family member, professor, or supervisor, may have an easier time understanding you than someone who has never met you. Therefore, the rating criteria is based on the *average person' ability* to understand the speaker. While raters can only assign each single test question an even score of 20, 30, 40, 50, or 60, mid scores of 25, 35, 45, and 55 occur for the final score based on the rounded average of the nine test questions (12 questions for SPEAK®).

Sample Responses

Now let's take a look at a typical question and some sample responses that represent different score levels.

> **Imagine that I am a college classmate of yours and would like to visit your home town. Suggest some place I should plan to see while I am visiting your town and explain why you think I would like to see it.** (30 seconds)

Response scored at 60

Well, I know you have an interest in architecture. Therefore, I recommend that you visit our town's historical society. They have a special exhibit about the architecture in our city. In the exhibit you will see photographs and models of various buildings of architectural significance in our city. I know you especially like seeing old blueprints, and they have plenty of those on display. You can easily spend a couple of hours viewing those exhibits.

The language function is clearly carried out, that is, the Historical Society is *recommended* because of the special architecture exhibit. The language appropriately takes into account the audience. The friend's interest in architecture in general, and in blueprints specifically, is addressed. Expressions like *well, plenty of,* and *a couple of* are informal and appropriate when speaking with a friend. The response is nicely organized because it begins with acknowledging the friend's interest in architecture, goes on to relate that to the Historical Society's architecture exhibit, and concludes with an estimate of how long it will take to view the exhibit. This response demonstrates good vocabulary such as *architectural significance* and *blueprints*. If this response were spoken fluently, with natural English rhythm, stress, and intonation, then it should receive a score of 60.

> Response scored at 50
>
> *Our city is famous for its museums. The best one ... One of my favorite ones are the Historical Society. I like the architecture exhibit. I think you would like it. The admission price ... It only costs about $3.00 for admission. They gave you a free map of an architectural walking tour. So after learning about the buildings you can take a tour. I mean follow the map and see these great buildings for yourself.*

Again the language function is clearly carried out, that is, the Historical Society is *recommended* because of the architecture exhibit. In fact, a second recommendation is made, and that is to take the walking tour. Making two recommendations does not in itself earn the speaker a higher score, but it does indicate that the speaker can communicate his ideas in a reasonable amount of time. Although the friend's interests are not taken into account as directly as in the level 60 response, the speaker does suggest that the friend will enjoy it because he himself enjoys it. The response is simply organized. It begins with museums in general, narrows to the Historical Society, and focuses on the architecture exhibit. Concrete examples like the $3.00 admission price and the walking tour map help to communicate the speaker's ideas. This response contains simple, but appropriate sentence structure and vocabulary such as *I like . . .* instead of *I have always been fascinated by . . . .* Notice that the speaker begins sentences and then starts over with an alternative phrasing. While this reduces fluency, it is not a major error that interferes with the communication. Also, the speaker mentions a tour, and then to clear up confusion, clarifies that it is a self-directed tour. There are a couple of grammar errors in verb tense as well, such as *one of my favorite ones are* instead of *is*, and *They gave you* instead of *give*. Imagine that the speaker pronounced some of his vowels incorrectly on words like *famous, cost, tour,* and *follow,* yet was generally understandable. If this response were otherwise spoken fluently, with natural English rhythm, stress, and intonation, then it should receive a score of 50.

> Response scored at 40
>
> *Yes, there are a building . . . a museum building. uh. This building is, uh, the Historic Societ. At this building, uh, there are the architecture exhibit. You will be interesting to see. There are pictures, uh, photos, uh, drawing, uh you know, of all the interesting buildings in my, uh city. OK? It is open until 5 p.m. You will be interesting to see.*

This type of response represents the middle-of-the-road answer, sometimes communicative, sometimes unclear. The language function of recommending with reasons is accomplished, but only after some effort. The speaker tries to consider his audience by suggesting that the friend will find the exhibit interesting, but the audience appropriacy is weakened by the awkward grammar and wording. There is little cohesion between sentences; along with the pausing and *uh* sounds, this makes for a choppy response. Simple grammar errors exist like *there is/are a building . . .* and *interested/ing*. Pronunciation is difficult to understand with the chopping off of word endings such as *Historical, Society,* and *drawings*. This response should be rated 40.

> Response scored at 30
>
> *OK, you would, uh, like, uh, to visit, uh, my home town. OK, OK, uh, my hometown is, uh, a big city. There is, uh, uh, a lot to do . . . in my , my city. Like museums.*

In this response the language function is only minimally carried out. While the speaker says her hometown is a big city and that there is a lot to do, she does not recommend visiting a specific place for specific reasons. Only at the end is the vague expression *Like museums* hastily mentioned. Because the speaker does not say much, the raters are not able to clearly assess whether the speaker is able to address the specific audience of a college classmate appropriately. The response is short, which also makes it difficult to rate coherence and cohesion. Content and details are lacking in this response. Sentences are short and of simple construction; the last phrase is not even a complete sentence. The unnecessary repetition of *OK* and the sound *uh* interfere with fluency and rhythm. Even if this response were spoken with good stress and intonation, it would be scored at 30.

Response scored at 20

Suggest some place I should plan to see . . .

This response is only the repetition of part of the question. The speaker does not create any language to be rated and therefore should be scored 20.

Response scored at 20

When you visit . . . I think you would like to see . . . In my hometown . . . Many places you visit.

This response does not address the language function of recommending with reasons; it does not address audience appropriateness; the incomplete sentences make it highly incoherent; and the fluency, rhythm, and vocabulary are weak. Therefore, a score of 20 would be assigned to this response as well.

It is important always to give some kind of response to each question. If you do not say anything at all or say something like, "Sorry, I don't know," then the raters will have no choice but to assign a score of 20 to that response. No matter what, it is important to respond to all of the questions. On the other hand, don't get upset if you don't give your best response to every question. There are nine questions that will be averaged into your final score. So concentrate on each question as it comes. The following chapters will provide you with advice and practice on how to maximize your communication abilities throughout the test.

–3–

Pronunciation

In this chapter you will

- Identify features that influence English pronunciation, including message units, alternations of stressed and unstressed syllables, primary stress, and intonation.
- Learn how the features of pronunciation interact in English.
- See examples of students' oral speech analyzed for pronunciation.
- Learn strategies for improving pronunciation.
- Practice English pronunciation.
- Identify pronunciation features that interfere with fluent English.

This excerpt comes from a talk given by a computer science teaching assistant (TA). Following the excerpt is the TA's written self-analysis.

EXCERPT

Today, I'll talk about rendering pipeline. Uh, in in our ordinary life, we use camera to capture the real world and display it in the photos. How can we do it in the computer and display the photo in the monitor screen? Uh, this process is called the rendering pipeline. At the first step, what we have to do is to model the real world.

SELF-ANALYSIS

In this talk I have several things to improve. First, my voice sounds monotonous. This problem is really hard to overcome. When I am talking, I never think of it. So it is difficult to improve. For example, when I said *in our ordinary life,* I should put primary stress on *life,* but I didn't do it. In my sentences, there are a few stresses.

Second, I had many improper pauses in my talk. Because I was choosing the proper words, I pause in the middle of the message units. I knew I shouldn't pause, but I didn't know what I should say.

Third, I had some grammar errors. I often mixed up the present tense and the past tense. In this talk, it was pretty good because it didn't have many past tenses. Also, I often omit *s* or *es* in my words *(pipelines, photos, lives, cameras).*

Fourth, I want to mention the content of my presentation. When I prepared the talk, I wanted to say something important. But when I gave the talk, I forgot to say it. For example, I wanted to explain what the modeling meant when preparing, but I forgot to do it in my real talk. This confused some people because I didn't explain it. Sometimes, I know I should say something, but I couldn't remember what it is. This was also one of the reasons of my pausing. When I tried to avoid the pause, I skipped the content and talked next point. Therefore, my real talk is faster than what I thought before.

Recording short talks not only allows you to practice speaking, but it provides an opportunity to analyze and improve your speaking ability. In this example, the student was able to identify specific areas for improvement, especially in linguistic accuracy (pronunciation, grammar, fluency, and vocabulary) and coherence. While it is valuable to receive feedback from experts, it can also be profitable to analyze your own speaking, as this example shows. This chapter provides information that will aid you in analyzing and improving your English pronunciation.

Pronunciation can be viewed from different levels, including the sound level, the word level, and the phrase level. Each level contributes to overall intelligibility, or how clearly others understand you. For example, vowel sounds change depending on whether they are stressed or not. Words are more understandable when the stressed syllables are clearly stressed and the unstressed syllables are clearly unstressed. Words are usually linked smoothly to other words in a phrase, and primary stress is placed on a word in a phrase that helps focus the listener.

This chapter focuses on English pronunciation at the phrase level. Message units, alternations of stressed and unstressed syllables, primary stress within a phrase, and intonation are all important pronunciation features at the phrase level. Concepts such as these should become clearer as you work through this chapter.

Quick Overview of Pronunciation

Here is a short passage from a TA teaching a lab in theoretical and applied mechanics.

> We're going to be plotting the hardness of this metal bar. Now, uh, the bar is basically a cylindrical metal specimen and it's . . . We're going to take it out of the oven and we're going to hold it in a bracket. So it's all going to be heated up to eight hundred and forty-five degrees Celsius.

Say this passage aloud. Do you feel comfortable with where you pause and what words you stress? Without accurate pausing and primary stress, it is difficult to get the other features of pronunciation correct. The passage is presented again with the message units marked with a / and the primary stress marked with bold, capital letters.

> We're going to be plotting the **HARD**ness of this metal bar / now / uh / the bar is basically a cylindrical metal **SPEC**imen and it's / . . . / we're going to take it out of the **OV**en / and we're going to hold it in a **BRAC**ket / so it's all going to be heated **UP** / to eight hundred and forty-five degrees **CEL**sius /.

More Detailed Overview of Pronunciation

Message Units

Phrases that are grouped together into meaningful units are called **message units,** thought groups, or phrases. There are common ways to form message units but generally no single correct way. A speaker usually groups together words that are meaningful. Some examples include:

- prepositional phrases
- clauses
- articles and adjectives with their nouns

Think about how you would divide the example sentence into message units.

> The final exam that was given last Tuesday will be
> graded by Monday or Tuesday of next week.

One speaker may divide this sentence into two message units:

> The final exam that was given last Tuesday / will be
> graded by Monday or Tuesday of next week.

Another speaker may divide the same sentence into four message units:

> The final exam / that was given last Tuesday / will be
> graded by Monday or Tuesday / of next week.

It would be inappropriate to create message units by pausing after *the* (such as *the / final*), in the middle of a word (such as *Tues / day*), or between *was* and *given*. All the sounds within a single message unit should flow together smoothly. This can be referred to as **linking.** Although written words have spaces between them, words spoken within a message unit have no breaks or pauses; they link together. The only breaks in sound come between message units. Message units add brief moments of silence in the flow of speech. This silence can add clarity to your language by expressing connections, emotions, or emphasis. Pausing can provide time for listeners to mentally process what is being said. If the meaning of even a phrase or two is lost, the listeners' mind may be searching for a way to fill in the missing phrases in a way that makes sense with the context. While this is occurring more phrases are being spoken. Even clearly spoken phrases that follow may be lost to the listeners if the listeners are too focused on the phrases they missed or if enough context was lost in the missed phrases to make the later phrases difficult to understand. Alternatively, inappropriate pausing can send negative signals. More frequent pausing can reflect strong feelings like irritation or excitement. Frequent pausing after individual words can draw attention away from what is important and leave the listener guessing about the real focus of the message.

Alternations

Message units are made of words, and words are made of syllables. Every syllable has a vowel, and one important function of the vowel is to carry the stress. Syllables are either stressed or unstressed. Stressed syllables are usually:

- Pronounced **longer** than unstressed syllables.
- Pitched **higher** than unstressed syllables.
- Spoken slightly **louder** than unstressed syllables.

These three features do not contribute equally to stress. Vowel length is generally the most critical of these features in indicating stress. So do not be fooled into thinking that saying stressed syllables louder is enough to carry the stress. For speakers who come from a language background where the tone is flatter than English, making stressed syllables louder may be easier than increasing the pitch or lengthening the vowel, but this is usually not enough to successfully indicate stress.

Pitch height can be thought of as varying along a continuum of heights. Alternations in the pitch create the melody of a language. Reaching for a specified pitch height is not the goal; rather a distinct contrast between the pitches of stressed and unstressed syllables is what is most helpful. In our example sentence, the stressed syllables are shown in bold letters. While syllables are composed of both consonants and vowels, remember it is the vowels that signal the degree of stress.

The final exam that was given last Tuesday will be
graded by Monday or Tuesday of next week.

The opposite of alternations would be constant pitch or nearly a flat tone across all syllables. A flat tone in English generally leaves a poor impression on the listener. This is because a flat tone makes it difficult to distinguish words and syllables. Listeners subconsciously depend on stress to highlight key ideas and new information; without this stress the listener may have to work harder to understand. Some listeners won't put this extra effort into listening and may stop listening or look for a way to end the conversation. Additionally, a flat tone may make the speaking rate seem too fast or too slow. What sounds like a fast speaking rate to the listener may be misinterpreted by that listener as though the speaker is in a rush, doesn't want to waste time on this, is upset, or excited. What sounds like a slow speaking rate to the listener may be misinterpreted as though the speaker is unsure, confused, or bored. On the other hand, stressing every other syllable whether it should be stressed or not creates what is called a sing-song effect and can annoy English listeners because words become difficult to interpret and main ideas become hidden.

Primary Stress

The focus of each message unit is marked by a strong stress called **primary stress** or **phrase stress**. There is generally only one primary stress within a message unit unless there is a comparison or contrast being emphasized. Primary stress is signaled by a movement in pitch and a vowel lengthening of the targeted syllable. It is most common for the pitch to rise for primary stress, though it could drop. In the example of a pitch rise, for the pitch to clearly mark primary stress, the pitch of the target syllable should be higher than all the other stressed syllables within that message unit. When primary stress is marked by a pitch rise and when it is marked by a pitch drop is not completely understood by researchers. Therefore, unless you have a natural tendency to use a pitch drop, you are encouraged to use the rise in pitch to mark primary stress in most situations. As you listen to native speakers of English, try to identify when a pitch drop is used for primary stress.

Frequently the primary stress falls on the last content word of new information. Nouns, verbs, adjectives, and adverbs are examples of content words. New information generally consists of words and ideas that have not been part of the conversation until that point. For example, if the conversation has been about an experiment, when the concept of completion date is introduced, that may be considered new information.

We hope to have our data collected by the end of the WEEK.

Although each word in the phrase *end of the week* may contain new information, it is just the last word of new information that generally carries the primary stress.

Speakers may deviate from the "last content word of new information" guideline if they choose to emphasize another word with primary stress to create a slightly different focus. In the example above, if the speaker wanted to emphasize the end of the week rather than earlier in the week, then the word end could carry the primary stress.

We hope to have our data collected by the END of the week.

The syllables within a message unit alternate between high and low pitch depending on whether the syllable is stressed or unstressed. There may be more than one unstressed syllable after another; likewise, there may be more than one stressed syllable adjacent to another. Think about how you would mark primary stress on this example sentence:

One last thing before we finish class, be sure to review chapter fifteen, especially the section on net present value.

First you want to divide the sentence into message units and then choose the syllable to carry primary stress for each phrase. Message units are marked with a /, stressed syllables are marked in **bold**, and the primary stress is marked with **BOLD CAPITAL** letters.

one last thing before we finish CLASS, / be sure to review chapter fifTEEN, / especially the section on net present VALue.

The guideline for placing stress on the last content word of new information suggests placing primary stress on the words *class, fifteen,* and *value.* There are times when function words, such as prepositions, negatives, question words, etc., carry primary stress when there are no content words within a message unit that convey new information.

Exercise 3.1: Analyzing Primary Stress

Primary stress is a valuable tool you possess to direct the listener's focus. Primary stress commonly falls on new information. Yet, you have the opportunity to place primary stress elsewhere. For example, primary stress can also be used to emphasize an important idea, a contrast with another concept, or an emotion. The sentences in this exercise come from a teaching assistant's observations of a class. In this exercise you will be given a sentence, and you will be asked to provide a reason for placing primary stress on various words. Consider each sentence as a single message unit for this exercise. The first one has been done for you.

1. I remember that visual system was one of the least interesting topics when I took Introduction to Psychology in college.

   a. *college:* <u>This is the last content word of new information.</u>

   _____

   b. *least:* <u>This emphasizes the speaker's lack of interest in</u>
      <u>this topic.</u>

   _____

   c. *I:* <u>This emphasizes the speaker's personal opinion or</u>
      <u>memory.</u>

   _____

   d. *visual:* <u>This emphasizes that the topic is visual system</u>
      <u>which is distinct and contrasts with some other type</u>
      <u>of system.</u>

   _____

2. All students could participate in the TA's interesting
   demonstrations.

   a. *participate:* _____

   _____

   b. *all:* _____

   _____

   c. *demonstrations:* _____

   _____

   d. *interesting:* _____

   _____

3. The TA asked students questions at appropriate times to encourage them to process the information more deeply.

    a. *deeply:* _____

    _____

    b. *more:* _____

    _____

    c. *process:* _____

    _____

    d. *encourage:* _____

    _____

4. The TA allowed enough wait time so students were given a chance to organize their thoughts before answering the question.

    a. *question:* _____

    _____

    b. *before:* _____

    _____

    c. *organize:* _____

    _____

    d. *enough:* _____

    _____

⬓ Exercise 3.2: Analyzing Primary Stress

Primary stress is not just a theoretical language concept; you can hear native speakers of English using primary stress all the time. Identify native speakers of English who you believe to have clear spoken English. You may find good examples of spoken English in some lectures, speeches, commercials, and newscasts. As you listen, note the words that receive primary stress, and think about what the speaker is focusing on by emphasizing these words. Remember, speakers can place primary stress on the last content word of new information in a phrase, or they may stress other words to convey some other emphasis.

Write three actual sentences you hear today. Mark the words that carry primary stress, and explain why you think the speaker chose to emphasize those words. Be sure to notice any facial expressions or gestures the speaker uses in conjunction with primary stress, and describe them. The first one has been done for you as an example.

Sentence 1: They have **said EXACTLY** what Doctor **Rinker said.**

Primary Stress: The word exactly carries the primary stress even though Rinker is the last content word of new information. By stressing exactly, the speaker may be conveying surprise that what was said by the group agrees so closely with what Dr. Rinker said. Or perhaps the speaker is happy that both statements are in agreement.

Gestures: The speaker's eyebrows rise up and his head nods slightly when he stresses the word exactly.

Sentence 2: _____

_____

Primary Stress: _____

_____

_____

_____

_____

Gestures: _____

_____

Sentence 3: _____

_____

Primary Stress: _____

_____

_____

_____

_____

Gestures: _____

_____

Sentence 4: _____

_____

Primary Stress: _____

_____

_____

_____

_____

Gestures: _____

_____

Intonation

Some people use the term **intonation** in a general sense to mean the rise
and fall in pitch of speaking. For example, if someone is referred to as a
monotone, it means intonation is flat in this general sense. There is a more
specific definition of intonation, which is referred to as intonation, intonation pattern, or intonation curve. In this specific definition, **intonation** describes the direction of the pitch after the primary stress. The three types of
specific intonation are:

- High range ➚
- Low range ➘
- Rise-to-mid range ⤴

Intonation is important because it conveys meaning that the words alone
cannot convey.

HIGH-RANGE INTONATION

High-range intonation is intonation that moves to a higher pitch. High range
is used for yes-no questions, repetition questions, information-seeking tag

questions, and statements that are asked as questions. Here is an example of a yes-no question with high-range intonation.

Do you want me to go over another EXAMple?

The sentence is short enough to be spoken as one message unit with linking between each word. The primary stress is placed on the **a** of *example,* and the intonation gains height over the letters *ple.*

In a conversation, the high-range intonation may mark a question and signal that it is the listener's turn to respond. If high-range intonation is placed on statements that are not intended to be questions, it may be misinterpreted that it is the listener's turn to begin speaking. Alternatively, the listener may get the impression that the speaker is uncertain, hesitant, or lacks confidence.

LOW-RANGE INTONATION

Low-range intonation is intonation that moves to a lower pitch. Low range is used for ending sentences, information questions, yes-no questions, comment tag questions, and on the last choice of choice question. An example of a choice question is below.

Do you want to meet with your group
at the beGINning / or END of class?

In the second message unit, the primary stress is on the word *end* and descends over the remaining words *of class.* This is an example of low-range intonation. (In the first message unit, the primary stress is shown on *-gin-* of *beginning,* and the intonation drops and rises slightly over *-ning.* This is an example of rise-to-mid-range intonation.)

When low-range intonation is used at the end of every phrase, it can be disturbing to the listener. Low-range intonation in the middle of a sentence will make it hard for the listener to associate related information together.

Constant use of low-range intonation can give the listener the impression that the speaker is angry, impatient, or rushed.

RISE-TO-MID-RANGE INTONATION

Rise-to-mid-range intonation is intonation that moves to the mid-range. When the primary stress is a pitch jump, rise-to-mid-range intonation begins by falling low and then rising to the mid-range. This is the most common form of rise-to-mid-range intonation because the pitch jump is the most common way to mark primary stress. (When the primary stress is a pitch drop, rise-to-mid-range intonation only requires a rise to the mid-range.) Rise-to-mid-range indicates the thought is not yet complete and that there is more information to come. Thus, rise-to-mid-range intonation is commonly found in message units that are not at the end of sentences. Here is an example.

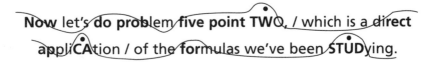

Rise-to-mid-range intonation occurs on the words *two* and *application*. If the pitch movement on the primary stress is a jump, then the rise-to-mid-range intonation falls and rises slightly to the mid-range. If the pitch movement on the primary stress is a drop, then the rise-to-mid-range intonation rises slightly to reach mid-range. Low intonation is used on the word *studying* in the third message unit since this completes the thought of the sentence.

When rise-to-mid-range intonation is used at the end of sentences, it can confuse the listener. Rise-to-mid-range intonation suggests that more related information is coming. After inappropriate rise-to-mid-range intonation, a listener may not take a turn to speak in a conversation believing that the other person has more to say. The speaker then may wonder why the listener is not responding. Alternatively, the use of rise-to-mid-range intonation at the ends of sentences may prompt the listener to try to look for a closer relationship between sentences than is meant to be. This wasted effort may distract or confuse the listener. Constant use of rise-to-mid-range intonation can give the listener the impression that the speaker is unsure, scared, or unprepared.

🔄 Exercise 3.3: Analyzing Intonation

*For each phrase, indicate what type of intonation would be appropriate by marking: **H** for high range, **L** for low range, **RM** for rise-to-mid-range. Say each phrase aloud with the appropriate intonation.*

Hi, John. (1)_____ I just heard that you're opening a computer store. (2)_____ Congratulations! (3)_____ You told me last year (4)_____ you were going to start a business. (5)_____ I'm really interested in looking at the computers, (6)_____ monitors, (7)_____ and software (8)_____ you have for sale. (9)_____ When will you be free to talk about computers? (10)_____ Can we meet Thursday (11)_____ or Friday? (12)_____ Let's plan to meet Friday afternoon, (13)_____ ok?

Pronunciation Analysis

Here is an excerpt from a computer science student's explanation about sorting. Message units and primary stress are marked. An analysis of this speech follows the excerpt.

EXCERPT

And today / I want to talk about two other / sorting **AL**go-rithm / and one is **BUB**ble sort / and another is **MERGE** sort / there are only two basic oper**A**tion in bubble sort / that / is com**PARE** / and **SWAP** / after **ONE** pass / we can see the

LARgest number / ar**RIVE** the correct position / just like the **BUB**ble / in the **WA**ter / the bubble will **FLOAT**ing up in the water / because / when we **MERGE** / if / the group is **SORT**ed / and we can merge / the **TWO** group / by checking the **FIRST** element of each group /

Analysis

Message units: First look at the message units. In general, grammatical phrases are used for message units. However, there is no need to pause between *other* and *sorting,* or between *that* and *is.* Additionally, it may also sound more fluent to link *merge* and *the* without the pause. The word *because* has pausing before and after, which is quite common as long as primary stress with mid-to-rise intonation is used. It would be better to pause before and not after the word *if.*

Primary stress: Primary stress is missed on only a few of the message units. A longer word, like *algorithm,* receives primary stress on the correct syllable. However, a word like *algorithm* should not carry the primary stress since it is part of a compound where the word *sorting* should be stressed. Primary stress is used nicely to highlight the contrast between *bubble sort* and *merge sort* and to emphasize the two alternatives *compare* and *swap.*

Intonation: The speaker used a flat choppy tone across the phrase *there are only two basic operation in bubble sort.* This could be improved by alternating pitch between stressed and unstressed syllables and by linking each of the words together to create a smooth flow of sound.

Cohesion: This student can also be encouraged to watch out for overuse of the connector *and.* The *ands* before *today* and *one is bubble sort* can be eliminated altogether. Using a variety of connector words and choosing them appropriately can improve cohesion.

Sounds: A number of *-s* endings are missing as well. This may be due to grammar, or it may be due to a pronunciation habit of dropping word endings. *S* could be added to words like *algorithm, operation, arrive,* and *group.*

Wording: This speech might also be improved by rewording some of the phrases for clarity. For example, *after one pass* may be more accurately stated as *after the first pass.* The analogy to a bubble floating up in the water is a helpful word picture but could be reworded slightly for enhanced clarity.

Overall: In this talk the student was effective in communicating some basic principles of his topic. The analysis mentions some areas where the student can improve. Even a native speaker delivering a talk could find areas for improvement. The goal is not to be perfect or error free but to maximize the communication as much as possible. It is helpful to analyze short speeches of your own, as well as to get feedback from friends or an ESL instructor.

For further information and practice on pronunciation, please refer to *Speechcraft: Discourse Pronunciation for Advanced Learners* (Hahn and Dickerson 1998).

---

⑤ Exercise 3.4: Analyzing Pronunciation Features

In each of the following excerpts, mark the pronunciation features as indicated and read the passage aloud. When these words are spoken clearly, they are grouped together into meaningful message units. Within each message unit all the syllables are linked smoothly together as they are spoken with the pitch alternating up and down for stressed and unstressed syllables. There is one primary stress within each message unit and intonation following each primary stress that is either high range, low range, or rise-to-mid-range. After marking the passage, read it aloud to a friend for feedback, or record your speech and analyze it yourself.

> Message unit: /
> Stressed syllables: ′
> Unstressed syllables: ˘
> Primary stress: •
> High-range intonation: (H)
> Low-range intonation: (L)
> Rise-to-mid-range intonation: (RM)

1. An excerpt from a theoretical and applied mechanics lab
The cylindrical bar/is going to be heated up to 845 degrees Celsius./And then/we're going to start/spraying water on the

bottom of it. So water will be hitting the bottom of the specimen. So . . . , the bottom of the cylindrical specimen will be cooled the quickest, and then you know as the water has a chance to take the heat away from the specimen, you know it's going to cool, y'know, gradually, as it goes up to the top.

Analysis

Message units: _____

_____

_____

Primary stress: _____

_____

_____

Intonation: _____

_____

_____

Wording: _____

_____

_____

Overall: _____

_____

_____

2. An excerpt from a civil engineering class in transportation

Today I'm going to talk about traffic signal operation. Uh, basically, traffic signal operation is, is divided into three different modes: retimed mode, actuated mode, and traffic responsive mode. If you, if you don't see any traffic detector on an intersection, you can assume that the traffic operation mode there is retimed traffic operation. These intersections are being operated based on a pre-programmed way. The major advantage of this operating mode is to make vehicle movement smooth when vehicles move through several intersections.

Analysis

Message units: _____

_____

_____

Primary stress: _____

_____

_____

Intonation: _____

_____

_____

Wording: _____

_____

_____

Overall: _____

_____

_____

3. An excerpt from an economics class

In microeconomics the behavior of consumers and firms are discussed and the . . . , in . . . , and different market structures. Therefore, it's a low level, actually, it's a micro level of economics. And macroeconomics discusses about the relation between the main factors of an economy, such as inflation or unemployment and interest rates and the effects of different economical policies such as monetary policy or fiscal policy on these parameters.

Analysis

Message units: _____

_____

_____

Primary stress: _____

_____

_____

Intonation: _____

_____

_____

Wording: _____

_____

_____

Overall: _____

_____

_____

4. An excerpt from a computer science class

In 1971, Intel released the first microprocessor. The microprocessor was a specialized integrated circuit which was able to process four bits of data at a time. The chip included its own arithmetic logic unit, but a sizable portion of the chip was taken up by the control circuits for organizing the work, which left less room for the data-handling circuitry.

Analysis

Message units: _____

_____

_____

Primary stress: _____

_____

_____

Intonation: _____

_____

_____

Wording: _____

_____

_____

Overall: _____

_____

_____

5. An excerpt from a theoretical and applied mechanics discussion session

So how do we find the mo . . . the force? um, well, what I've, I've already imagined that there are some forces acting in order to keep this bar back. This guy (piece) is rotating, right? This is just like the little spiel (explanation) I gave about the bucket at the beginning of class. And so if I take a bucket of water and spin it around my head, my shoulder has to apply a certain amount of force to keep this bucket from flying away, right?

Analysis

Message units: _____

_____

_____

Primary stress: _____

_____

_____

Intonation: _____

_____

_____

Wording: _____

_____

_____

Overall: _____

_____

_____

Exercise 3.5: Developing a Short Talk

Develop a short 3–5 minute talk, about something related to your discipline. A list of suggestions is provided to help you start thinking of a topic. Select a topic and create an outline. Rehearse your talk aloud. When you are ready, record your talk.

1. Discuss an important person—someone who has made an impact on your field of study.

2. Discuss an important invention in your field of study.

3. Discuss an important event in your discipline.

4. Discuss an important place in your discipline.

5. Explain a basic concept in your discipline.

6. Compare and contrast two terms in your discipline.

7. Explain a procedure in your discipline.

8. Discuss some of the research methods used in your discipline.

9. Describe how to use a piece of equipment that is used in your discipline.

10. Describe some of the jobs common to your discipline.

11. Discuss a current event or news story that relates to your discipline.

12. Discuss opportunities for interdisciplinary research with your discipline.

Self-Analysis

After recording your talk, analyze your pronunciation. To analyze your talk effectively, follow these steps:

1. Transcribe your talk, which means write down every word and sound that you spoke, including *ums* and *uhs.*

2. Mark the pronunciation features, including where you paused for message units, primary stress, alternations, and intonation.

3. Examine your marked transcript. Make a list of what you did well and another list of what you can improve.

4. Practice your talk and record it again. Listen for improvements.

➡ Tips for AVOIDING DISFLUENCIES

If fluency can be described as smooth, flowing, effortless speech, then disfluencies are anything that interfere with fluency. The most common disfluencies that stem from pronunciation difficulties include:

_____ • Speaking word by word rather than phrase by phrase.

_____ • Inaccurate word stress.

_____ • Flat tone instead of alternating pitches between stressed and unstressed syllables.

_____ • Not marking phrase stress with vowel lengthening and pitch movement.

_____ • Not linking sounds between words within a phrase, and in consonant clusters.

_____ • Using low-range intonation instead of rise-to-mid-range intonation at the end of message units at mid-sentence.

_____ • Inappropriate use of high-range intonation.

_____ • Mouth too closed instead of opening wide for many American English sounds.

_____ • Inaccurate pronunciation of vowels and consonants in key terms.

_____ • Speaking too fast.

These disfluencies are to be avoided not only because they don't mimic the speech patterns of native English speakers, but because they can interfere with communication. Listeners may not know which information to focus on and what ideas are related to one another. Additionally, listeners may inadvertently interpret some disfluencies as signs of anger, uncaring, boredom, or bossiness when these were not the intended messages. Clear pronunciation takes focused practice, yet the potential benefits are tremendous. Improved pronunciation can often lead to easier and more in-depth communication. Of the disfluencies noted, check one that occurs frequently in your speech. Focus on improving this disfluency as you work on the practice exercises in this book and as you communicate in general.

— PART 2 —

The New TSE® Test

–4–

A Sample Test

In this chapter you will:

- Become familiar with the instructions for the TSE® Test.
- Become familiar with the types of questions on the TSE® Test.
- Become familiar with the time allotted for responses on the TSE® Test.
- See sample questions that will be discussed in further detail in later chapters.

There is no way to predict the exact questions you will receive on the TSE®; nevertheless, the directions and format of the TSE® are standardized. Every test will have three warm-up questions followed by nine questions that will be organized similar to this:

1. Narrate a story. *cinderella*
2. Discuss advantages and disadvantages.
3. Share an opinion. *Gay marriage*
4. Discuss a hypothetical situation.
5. Describe a graph.
6. Analyze a graph.
7. Extend a greeting.
8. Respond to a phone message.
9. Give a progress report.

Understanding the format of the test can help reduce your anxiety about the questions you might be asked on the test. A sample test follows.

Review the directions and the questions. When you are ready to take the test for practice, record your own responses to the test. The chapters that follow will discuss each of the questions and numerous sample responses. Compare your responses to what you read in the chapters, and try to identify communication strategies that you can improve.

— Sample Test 1 —

(ID# = 57-8319)

This test is designed to help you practice for the TSE® Test. Record your answer to each response. Remember to speak directly into the microphone of your recording device. There are time limits following each question. The test narrator will let you know when to start and stop talking. Do your best to answer as well as you can within the stated time limit. The total test time will be about 20 minutes. These questions are not intended to measure your knowledge of any particular field, but to provide a context so that your communicative ability can be evaluated.

The next few questions are given as a warm-up. They ask simple questions about you. Do your best to give complete answers to each of these questions.

1. What is the number on the top of your test? (10 seconds)
2. When did you begin studying English? (10 seconds)
3. Why did you decide to take this test? (10 seconds)

That completes the warm-up question section, and now the actual test begins. For each question, try to be as clear as possible and to respond as completely as you can.

In this section of the test, you will see six pictures that depict a story line. You will be given 60 seconds to review the pictures. After that, you will be asked to tell the short story that is illustrated by the pictures. Try to include all six pictures in your story. I will let you know when to begin telling the story. (preparation time = 60 seconds)

1. Here are six pictures that illustrate a short story. Starting at the beginning, tell me the complete story picture by picture. (60 seconds)

2. In this picture sequence you see a person riding a bicycle. Some people get around by using bicycles while other people use cars. Pretend that you are talking to someone who has just arrived in the United States and tell them about the pros and cons of bicycles and cars as transportation. (60 seconds)

The next few questions will ask you about your thoughts on a number of different issues. Feel free to think for a couple seconds before you begin answering. Try to answer as thoroughly as you can in the time given for each question.

3. Many large cities like Baltimore, Chicago, and Seattle have aquariums where people can view sea animals. However, some people think that sea animals should not be taken out of nature and forced to live in small aquarium tanks. Please tell me your opinion about this question. (60 seconds)

4. If you were given a million dollars to donate to one charity, what charity or type of charity would you give it to? (60 seconds)

Here is a graph of State University's enrollment over two decades. You now have 15 seconds to review the graph. (preparation time = 15 seconds)

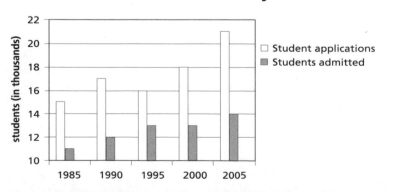

Enrollment for State University

5. Please tell me about the information portrayed in this graph. (60 seconds)

6. Please propose some reasons that may explain the data shown in the graph. (60 seconds)

For the next three questions, you are to pretend that you work in a business setting or are talking with someone about business. These situations provide you with an opportunity to demonstrate how well you can converse in a business environment. Your response should be suitable for addressing the people and context provided in the situation of each question. You may find it helpful to take notes as you listen.

7. In this situation you will be asked to talk with a business associate. Pretend that your business associate has just recently started his or her own business. Greet your business associate and be sure to:

- say something about the new business,
- say something positive regarding the new business, and
- offer appropriate wishes to the business associate.

Use the next 30 seconds to prepare your response. I will indicate when you should begin speaking. (preparation time = 30 seconds)

You may begin your response now. (60 seconds)

8. In this situation you will hear and respond to a telephone message containing a complaint. Pretend that you are the manager of an apartment rental company. After the message is played, you will have 30 seconds to think about a response. Your response should:

- demonstrate that you understand the caller's problem, and
- suggest a solution to the problem that would satisfy the caller.

Please listen to the voice message. (On the TSE® the voice message will be played aloud. It will not be written as it is here.)

··

Hello. My name is Ellen Harrison. Last week I moved into apartment B in the Green Street Apartments. I was told that the loose tiles on the kitchen floor and the leaky faucet in the bathroom would be fixed within three days. The repairperson came yesterday to fix the tiles, and it looks really nice. But I haven't seen the plumber yet, and the dripping from the faucet is driving me crazy at night when I am trying to sleep. Please call me back today, and let me know how you're going to take care of this. I tried calling all weekend but kept getting your answering machine. The leak is getting worse everyday, and I don't want to have to worry about this problem anymore.

··

You may now take 30 seconds to think about your response to the caller. I will tell you when you can start recording your response. (preparation time = 30 seconds)

Please begin your response now. (60 seconds)

9. Along with seeing a flow chart you will hear a conversation between two people. Based on that information, you will be asked to make an oral progress report as if you were leaving a voice-mail message on the telephone. Pretend that you work in the human resource division of an organization that is going through the hiring process. You will have the next 15 seconds to review the flowchart that outlines the hiring process. (preparation time = 15 seconds)

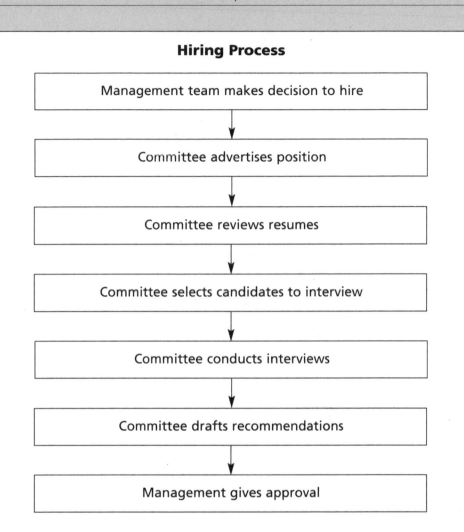

Hiring Process

Management team makes decision to hire

↓

Committee advertises position

↓

Committee reviews resumes

↓

Committee selects candidates to interview

↓

Committee conducts interviews

↓

Committee drafts recommendations

↓

Management gives approval

In a moment you will hear two people talking about the company hiring process. When the conversation is completed, you will have 45 seconds to prepare a voice-mail progress report for your supervisor, Mr. Richland. Please listen to the conversation. (On the TSE® the dialogue will be played aloud. It will not be written as it is here.)

....

Maria: Hi, Andrew! Have you made any progress on filling that job opening?

Andrew: You wouldn't believe it; it's been quite a job. That committee takes up more of my time than anything else right now.

Maria: Did many people apply?

Andrew: Exactly! That's part of the problem. We received over 100 resumes, and each committee member had to review each one. It took forever, but we finally narrowed it down to three candidates.

Maria: When will the interviews be?

Andrew: Actually, we held two of the interviews yesterday, and the third one is on Friday. I've been in charge of arranging to give each candidate a company tour, so I've gotten to know each one fairly well so far.

Maria: When will a final decision be made?

Andrew: The committee will meet early next week to prepare a recommendation for the management team. If everything goes smoothly, we should have a new worker on the job before the busy season starts.

Maria: That would be great. I bet you'll be happy when this process is over.

Andrew: I've learned a lot during the process, but I'll definitely be glad when it's over.

....

Use the next 45 seconds to prepare your report for Mr. Richland. In your report be sure to:

- describe what the situation is,
- explain what has been accomplished, and
- report what is left to be done.

Do not begin your progress report voice-mail until you are instructed to do so. (preparation time = 45 seconds)

You may begin your response now. (60 seconds)

End of sample test

–5–

Warm-Up Questions

In this chapter you will:

- Learn about the purpose of the warm-up section of the TSE®.
- See examples of warm-up questions and responses.
- Learn what makes an effective response to warm-up questions.
- Practice responding to practice warm-up questions.

The general directions for the warm-up section of the test will be something like this:

The next few questions are given as a warm-up. Your responses to these questions will not be scored. They ask simple questions about you. Do your best to give complete answers to each of these questions.

While this section of the TSE® is not rated, it is an important part of the test. Although raters are instructed not to listen to this section of the test, it provides you with an opportunity to warm up your voice and to become comfortable speaking into the recording equipment. By starting off strongly on this warm-up section, you will build up your confidence and be more at ease during the remainder of the test. On the other hand, if you mumble or falter on an answer during the warm-up, don't worry about it. The whole point is to get you ready, so it's better to get your nervousness out in the warm-up section so you can do your best on the rated portion of the TSE®.

This section of the test includes three simple and straightforward questions. Since you will only have ten seconds to answer each question, your answers should be simple and straightforward as well. Do not try to say too much. Try to say enough when answering the question to demonstrate you know how to say what you want to say and thereby build your confidence.

Warm-Up Question 1

The first question of the warm-up section may be something like this:

What is the ID number on the label of your test?
(10 seconds)

When you respond to this question, give a short, complete sentence. You may even want to repeat the number for clarity. For an ID number of 4320, an example response would be:

The number is four thousand three hundred and twenty, four-three-two-zero.

Although this response is short, it sounds fluent because it answers the question directly in a complete sentence and focuses on the important information.

⬡ Exercise 5.1: Saying Numbers

To further prepare for this section, practice saying numbers by counting from:

- *0 to 10 by ones*
- *10 to 100 by tens*
- *100 to 1,000 by hundreds*
- *1,000 to 10,000 by thousands*

Note that when pronouncing thousand, *use a voiceless /th/ sound as in* thin, think, *and* theory.

⬡ Exercise 5.2: Saying Four-Digit Numbers

When a noun does not follow a number, the primary stress goes on the last stressed syllable (see Hahn and Dickerson 1998). For example, in 8,347 the first syllable of seven (sev) *is given primary stress. Practice saying four-digit numbers like these with the stress on the underlined part:*

8,347	9,752	3,972	5,689	2,780	4,193
7,248	6,556	3,327	2,050	5,948	8,288
2,190	1,643	6,191	3,801	4,824	7,899

The first warm-up question frequently asks about the number on the test booklet. So you should be prepared for that specific question in case it is asked. When you first receive your test booklet, make sure you locate the number on the cover. Use the brief time before the test begins to think about how to say the identification number. Pronounce it to yourself silently. In this way you will be prepared for the first question even before it is asked. This will increase your confidence and help you maximize your speaking performance.

Warm-Up Question 2

The second question of the warm-up section may be something like this:

> ## When did you begin studying English? (10 seconds)

The TSE® is supposed to measure the *way* you say your answer, not the actual answer. Yet raters are human, so it is important to make a good impression on the rater from the beginning. Therefore, you should speak confidently and fluently to communicate your response to the given question. As stated before, when you respond to this question, give a short, complete sentence. It is not essential to give the exact amount of time in months or years. You can use words like *almost* and *approximately* to qualify your answer. An example response is:

> ## *I began studying English approximately five years ago.*

Often it is helpful to use the stem of the question to begin your answer. For example, the question asks *When did you begin . . .* , so the answer starts off with *I began . . . .* This helps to promptly produce responses that are complete, fluent sentences.

You don't need to elaborate on your answer by explaining whether you have studied English in school or on your own, or whether you have studied in your home country or in the United States. Additional information could bias the rater's judgment, so be careful about supplying information that is not specifically asked for in the question. By trying to add additional information in your response, you increase the opportunity for errors. Likewise, you may find it hard to finish in ten seconds and end up being cut off. This will likely result in sounding incoherent. Rather, a short, complete answer sounds fluent and shows that you are in control of your language.

⟲ Exercise 5.3: Evaluating Responses

Now look at ten different responses to this question. Decide which are the five best responses, and place a check mark by them. Compare your check marks with a partner. Discuss with a partner what you liked about the responses you checked and how the responses you didn't mark could be improved.

_____ 1. It was approximately seven years ago when I first enrolled in English classes.

_____ 2. I began studying English when I was in high school. I took English classes at a private English institute after school. Since then I have studied English in college for four years, and I continue to study English on my own.

_____ 3. I have never studied English formally; what I know I have learned mostly from self-study and by watching TV.

_____ 4. I began studying English when I was a high school student.

_____ 5. I have studied English for about ten years, mostly grammar and vocabulary.

_____ 6. I seriously began studying English as an exchange student in North America when I was in high school.

_____ 7. I began studying English about six years ago, but for the last two years I really have not practiced my English much.

_____ 8. When I was a child I traveled a lot with my parents to English-speaking countries. Since that time I have been studying and learning English.

_____ 9. I began taking English classes in elementary school, but did not seriously begin to study English until my senior year of college.

_____ 10. Since I was a child, all of my schooling has been conducted in English.

Warm-Up Question 3

The third question of the warm-up section may be something like this:

Why did you decide to take this test? (10 seconds)

When responding, do not deviate from the question and do not supply information that is not asked for. As with warm-up question 2, you do not want to bias the rater's opinion of you if the rater accidentally heard the responses to the warm-up questions. Do not indicate whether this is the first or fifth time you are taking the TSE®. Raters are trained to focus on how you speak and to not be influenced by the content of your response; however, raters don't want to or need to know if other raters have scored you low in the past and caused you to retake the test. Also, be careful to frame your response in a positive way rather than a negative way. Do not tell the rater you are forced to take this test by your university, or that you are afraid you will not get a certain job if you don't pass the test. Respond in a positive way. For example:

> *I must pass this test before I can study at an American university.*

or

> *This test is required to become licensed in my field.*

This type of answer communicates confidence and directly answers the question asked. Short, complete answers convey fluency and control of language.

Warm-Up Practice Questions

These practice questions will help you prepare to think quickly and respond concisely to warm-up questions. Work on one practice set at a time. If you preview all the questions at once, you will ruin the spontaneity. Make your practice as realistic as possible by not looking ahead at other questions and by keeping to the time limit. For each set of questions, record your responses. Then listen to each response to see if you have answered concisely, fluently, and positively. Correct and repeat responses that need improvement before going on to the next practice set.

Practice Questions 5.1

- What is your social security number? (10 seconds)
- How long have you been waiting for the test to begin? (10 seconds)
- Why did you bring a watch with you? (10 seconds)

Practice Questions 5.2

- What is your telephone number? (10 seconds)
- How long did it take you to get to the test center? (10 seconds)
- Why did you decide to wear those clothes today? (10 seconds)

Practice Questions 5.3

- What is your driver's license number? (10 seconds)
- How long have you owned your watch? (10 seconds)
- Why did you leave your calculator at home today? (10 seconds)

Remember, the warm-up section is not rated, so use it to get off to a good start for the remainder of the test.

–6–

Narrate a Story

In this chapter you will:

- Become familiar with the instructions for *narrate a story* questions of the TSE®.
- See examples of *narrate a story* questions and corresponding responses.
- Learn what makes an effective response to *narrate a story* questions.
- Practice responding to a variety of *narrate a story* questions.

The general directions for the picture section of the test may be something like this:

In this section of the test, you will see six pictures that depict a story line. You will be given 60 seconds to review the pictures. After that, you will be asked to tell the short story that is illustrated by the pictures. Try to include all six pictures in your story. I will let you know when to begin telling the story. (preparation time = 60 seconds)

Use the 60 seconds to study the pictures. During that time you should think of nouns, verbs, adjectives, and adverbs that are appropriate for the scene, people, and action depicted. Accurate use of pronouns is extremely important for your listeners to understand what you are saying. Since the pronouns *he* and *she* can be potentially confusing to some non-native speakers of English, you may want to identify the characters with simple names like *Bob* and *Beth* or with descriptions like *the police officer* or *the bus driver*. The story usually will show some kind of conflict or problem, so take a few seconds to think about a clear way to describe the problem. It can be helpful to imagine what the characters are thinking and feeling as you prepare to tell the story.

Do not try to memorize specific phrases to use in your response. Instead of helping you to sound fluent, these generally have the effect of sounding unnatural and inappropriate. For example, do not start your story with *once upon a time*, or *an analysis of these six pictures reveals*. The first is only appropriate for a fairy tale, and the second sounds too formal for a narration. It would be better to begin the story by focusing on the specific scene or characters.

If you are taking the new TSE®, paper and pencil will be available. While they are intended for use with questions that have a listening portion, you may use them on this and other questions. Since time is limited, it is recommended that you don't use your time writing notes for this question. It is probably better to organize your ideas in your mind and allow the pictures to guide your thoughts.

When the minute to review the pictures is over, you may be asked something like this:

> **Here are six pictures that illustrate a short story. Starting at the beginning, tell me the complete story picture by picture.** (60 seconds)

It is recommended that you first decide if you will tell the story in past or present tense. Whichever tense you choose, be sure you stick with it through the entire story. There are times when native speakers of English will switch tense within a narrative. This can occur if the narrative becomes complex or when fine points are distinguished, so you may hear tense shifting from speakers during narratives (Celce-Murcia and Larsen-Freeman,

City Park

Bike Rentals

1 Hour = $ 5
2 Hours = $10
3 Hours = $13

1

2

Bike Rentals

3

4

Bike Rentals

5

6

1983, 66–67). However, for the purposes of the TSE® or other simple narratives, you may find it easier to stick with past or present tense.

For some people it is helpful to take on the role of the main character in the story and to tell the story as if it were about themselves. Other people like to describe what they see in the pictures. You should decide which perspective you prefer. Don't spend too much time on any one picture. Your words should concentrate on the major idea shown in each picture. You can assume that the rater is looking at the pictures while listening to you. An example response to this question is:

> *It was a sunny day, and John was walking through the park. Because it was hot John was wearing shorts and a t-shirt. There were beautiful trees along the path, and John saw boats sailing on the lake. Off to the side he saw a booth where someone was renting bicycles. John liked bike riding and decided it would be nice to take a bike ride through the park. So he gave the cashier at the booth five dollars to rent a bike for one hour. At first John enjoyed his bike ride. He enjoyed the breeze in his face as he rode along the bike path. In a short time John traveled a long way on his rented bike. Suddenly John hit a sharp rock with his front tire. The wheel went flat, and John was no longer able to ride the bike. Sadly, John walked the bike back to the booth. He was hot and tired by the time he reached the booth.*

This answer uses basic past tenses throughout the story such as: *was, was walking, were, saw, was renting, liked, decided, gave, enjoyed, rode, traveled, hit, went, walked,* and *reached.* Since the story can be clearly communicated without using a variety of complex past tenses, it is easiest to stick with basic past tenses. The main character is given the name John. The other man is identified by his job of cashier. Notice that key action words are used to describe the pictures, like *walking, renting, enjoyed,* and *hit.* Key adjectives are used to describe only selected ideas suggested from the pictures, like *sunny day, beautiful trees,* and *sharp rock.* Insignificant details are not mentioned such as the rabbit under the tree, or the number of bikes next to the booth. There is not enough time to talk about these minor details, and they would tend to distract the rater from understanding your primary message.

Cohesion is achieved through the use of expressions like *because* and *so. Because it was hot . . . ,* provides a transition from the weather in the scene to what the main character was wearing. *So he gave the cashier . . .* provides a transition from the statement that John likes bike riding to his actual renting of a bike. Cohesion can express new ideas, additional ideas, cause, effect, and contrast (Wennerstrom 1989). Cohesive devices are critical in making your ideas flow together in a logical order that communicates clearly to the rater.

⟳ Exercise 6.1: Using Cohesive Devices

Now let's practice using cohesive words and expressions. Here are pairs of words. There are a number of ways to connect each pair. Write out at least three different ways. The first example has been done for you.

1. Tom . . . feel sick

   Tom . . . attend a party

   <u>Although Tom feels sick, he still plans on attending the</u>
   <u>party.</u>

   <u>Because Tom was feeling sick, he decided not to attend</u>
   <u>the party.</u>

   <u>While attending the party, Tom started to feel sick.</u>

2. Brianna . . . tired out

   Brianna . . . take a vacation

   _____

   _____

   _____

3. Julie . . . hungry

   Julie . . . go to a restaurant

   _____

   _____

   _____

4. Mark . . . research

   Mark . . . meet deadline

   _____

   _____

   _____

5. Connie . . . graduate

   Connie . . . look for a job

   _____

   _____

   _____

Here is an alternative response to this question that is more informal in tone and utilizes the first person pronoun *I*.

> *It was Saturday afternoon, and I decided to take a walk through the park. It was the end of the spring semester, and I felt like I needed some fresh air and exercise. Pretty soon I saw a new bicycle rental place. I thought to myself, "It sure would be nice to go for a bike ride on such a beautiful day." So I paid the cashier and went for a ride. At first I enjoyed seeing the beautiful scenery while biking. Then suddenly, I hit a sharp rock with the front tire of the bike. The wheel went flat immediately. I couldn't ride it, and I had no way of fixing it. Sadly, I pushed the bike all the way back to the rental place in the hot sun. I had wanted to relax, but I ended up frustrated.*

Here is another example response to this same question. You will see the symbol ə, called schwa, in the first line which indicates an *uh* sound.

> *Last ə Sunday morning / Mr. Smith went to the city park / for refreshment / he want - ed to go on the park / but / this time he decided to try new way / he went to the / bike / rentals department in the park / and axed [asked] for whether he could / rent a park / uh / rent a bike / going along the park / then / the serviceman / told him that / there were / three choices / there / there was three choices / Mr. Smith / got / got one / and he payed a bucks for the bike rentals / then he / uh rode / he rode the bicycle / around the park / and it / took a long time / however / finally he found out / the frontal / wheel of the / the front tire of the bicycle was broken*

This response starts by setting the time, *Sunday morning*, the character, *Mr. Smith*, and the place, *the city park*. The speaker monitors his own language output. After he mistakenly said *rent a park*, he quickly changed it to *rent a bike*. Unfortunately, he also changed *there were three choices* to the incorrect form of *there was three choices*. It is acceptable to correct yourself while speaking during the test, but remember that the raters rate the last thing spoken. So don't continually second guess and change your wording unnecessarily.

The wording of this response is generally clear. Choosing the correct preposition can be difficult at times. The phrase *he wanted to go on the park* could be reworded to *he wanted to go through the park* or *he wanted to see the park*. The phrase *going along the park* could be changed to *going through the park* or *ride through the park*. *Bucks* is used informally for money but should be linked with a dollar amount like *eight bucks*. *Frontal wheel* could simply be referred to as *front wheel*. In narrating a story, it is acceptable to use informal language, but make sure your phrasing is precise enough to communicate clearly to the listener.

One pronunciation problem that many speakers deal with is linking or connecting words when the first ends in a consonant and the adjacent word begins with a consonant. This can be seen in the first phrase of the response *last Sunday*. The speaker adds an *uh* sound, symbolized by ə, after the final consonant cluster *st* of last and before the beginning consonant *s* of Sunday. This is a common problem for people coming from languages that have a consistent consonant-vowel-consonant-vowel pattern. Some speakers accidentally add *uh* between adjacent consonants to make English fit the pattern they are used to. Unfortunately, this extra syllable interferes with a listener's comprehension. Listen to yourself to find out if this is a concern for you. If so, you can practice by softening, or releasing less air, on a word's final consonants and linking directly to the adjacent word's initial consonants. In general, still try to form all the consonant sounds, just don't over-pronounce them. Exercise 6.2 will help you practice.

🔊 Exercise 6.2: Linking Practice

Practice linking sounds together within a message unit. Focus especially on linking the end consonant of one word to the beginning consonant of the next.

1. Next semester
2. right now
3. first reason
4. the last fifteen years
5. I think that because
6. three years to go
7. those books and papers
8. enrolled students
9. prescribed tests
10. message system

Here are a couple more example responses:

> *Today is Sunday / and it is a sunny day / Thomas decided to enjoy the day / and uh see the park / he / got up ear(ly) / in the morning / and he went to ther / park / and uh he went to ther / park rentals / ther / the the reasons (rates) for renting a / a bike is / uh one five dollars for one hour / ten dollars two hours / and uh / thirteen dollars / for three hours / he payed cash / uh to the bike owner / and he rented a bike and a helm(et) / and uh he began to ride on the road / around the / around the city park / a lot of people were . . .*

Notice that this speaker is frequently adding an /r/ sound to the word *the*. This problem usually happens to vowels that are pronounced while raising the tongue too high in the mouth. If this is a concern of yours, try to concentrate on your tongue position and keep it lower in your mouth when pronouncing vowels. Sometimes speakers add an /r/ sound when they are thinking. This is known as a filler sound. Since it does not add to meaning, try to avoid it.

It is Sunday / uh / it is it was a Sunday / uh / it was sunny / and slightly windy / so Peter thought it very nice to walk outside for awhile / so we so he went to the city park / in the park / he saw a man / rent a / rent bike / so he he he he thought that it it might be a good / be very good to / ride / ride a bike in the / park / so he / spent five dollars / to rent a pa bike for an hour / um / after he rode the bike / he felt so good / he enjoyed the sunlight / and uh / liked the wind very much / however / at this time / the bike / uh / the / the bike hit a / sh sharp rock / so he got a flat tile (tire)

In this response the word *so* is relied on for connections between phrases. *After*, *and*, and *however* are also used as connectors. Connector words and phrases help to keep the flow of the story moving and show the logical connection between events; however, it appears that *so* is used by the speaker here as a way to begin new sentences. The phrase *so Peter thought it very nice to walk outside* could be restated as *the nice weather motivated Peter to walk outside.* The phrase *so he went to the city park* could be restated as *to get away from the busy streets he decided to go to the park for a walk* or *he headed to the city park for a walk.* There are many times when phrases and sentences make stronger connections than single connection words like *so* and *and.*

The next two responses come from native speakers of English. One speaker uses the present tense, while the other uses past tense.

> *In uh picture one the guy is / walking through a city park / throws away some garbage / and then he sees a / a bike rental place / where he goes 'n / rents a bicycle / uh he pays the money to the guy / and uh / puts on his helmet and rides the bicycle / uh all through the park / then he finds as he's riding around that he gets a flat tire / and he returns it back to the guy um / who rented him the bicycle to figure out what went on / he doesn't look too happy* (25 seconds remaining)

> *A man decided to go to the park / and he walked into the park and threw away some trash on his way in / um / then he went and decided to rent a bike / so / um / he got a bike and / he paid the money for the bike / um / and / he began to ride around the park and he was really enjoying himself / then sadly / he got a flat tire / and he's very sad this is kind of upsetting to him so / he took the bike back to the bike rental / uh / uh person who / gave him the bike to ask for his money back / and for a new / uh bike tire / but uh the man / who / ehem / rented the bike to him didn't want to give him the money back* (0 seconds remaining)

The first response starts by referring to *picture one,* but since this is not the typical way of telling a story, the speaker abandons this strategy and focuses on telling the story without further reference to picture numbers. The first response doesn't use all the time allotted but still manages to convey the entire story. The second response includes more detail and fills the entire time. In these two responses it can be seen that even native speakers of English will use some filler sounds like *um.* However, the message units are fluent, and the intonation patterns appropriate so communication remains clear. Both speakers include the feelings of the character in the story: *he doesn't look too happy* and *he's very sad this is kind of upsetting to him.* The first speaker is a bit more informal using the words *guy* instead of *man,* and *'n* for *and.* Most of the sentences are short phrases. Connector words include *and, then, so, but,* as well as clauses like *who rented him the bicycle.*

Here is another sample response:

> *Okay / (clears throat) / one day Mr. Yohnso (Johnson) was walking in the park in the city park / and he decide instead of / walking / to rent a bike / so he went to the re bike rental / and pay for three hours here thirteen bucks / to the guy / to rent the bike / so / once that he rent the bike he was / traveling around the park / enjoying the life / it was a sunny day / but he hit a rock and / his wheel was destroyed so he went back to the bike rental and / tried to talk with the guy but the guy told him that / he can / he can not do anything because / it was no refun(d) for the money / (laugh) / so / that's a short story about / Mr. Johnson's / very nice Sunday / (laugh)*

This student uses longer phrases than most. At times this sounds fluent as in the phrase *his wheel was destroyed so he went back to the bike rental.* At other times, additional pausing may help make a longer phrase more understandable. For example, after *Mr. Johnson was walking in the park* there could be a pause before *in the city park* is added. Appropriate contrasting stress appeared on the word *city* to highlight the contrast between *park* and *city park.* This speaker had not seen the TSE® before and did not know what to anticipate. This uncertainty may have come out as the nervous laughs at the end of the response. Knowledge about the test and meaningful practice can help eliminate much of the nervousness that a test taker normally feels.

⑤ Exercise 6.3: Narrating a Scene

To practice narrating, turn on a TV show or a movie with the volume turned down all the way. Narrate the scene and action you see for five minutes. Do this daily for two weeks.

⑤ Exercise 6.4: Analyzing Your Narrating

Working with a partner, narrate what you did last weekend. Ask your partner for feedback on your communication. If you do not have a partner to work with, record your narration and analyze it yourself.

⑤ Exercise 6.5: Narrating a Story

Turn to the comics page of a newspaper. Without looking at the words, narrate the story that the pictures show.

➡ Tips for NARRATING A STORY QUESTIONS

1. Begin the story by setting the context. You can describe the time, place, and or people involved.
2. Be consistent with verb tense—for example, use simple past tense.
3. Choose names for the characters and clearly identify what you are calling each character.
4. If you use pronouns *he* and *she,* be careful to use them accurately.
5. You may want to pretend that you are one of the characters in the story. If so, clearly identify which character you are.
6. During the time given to study the pictures, think of verbs, nouns, and adjectives you can use in telling the story.
7. Try not to spend too much time on each picture. A sentence or two for each will fill up the 60 seconds.
8. If you finish slightly before the minute is over, don't force yourself to say more if you have nothing more to add.
9. Don't worry if you didn't complete the whole story. The raters will rate the language sample you did provide.
10. Let both words and the tone in your voice express the emotion of the story, such as excitement or frustration.
11. Pause in grammatical places. Link the sounds within any single phrase. Include primary stress on each phrase and alternate pitch between stressed and unstressed syllables. Use appropriate intonation for phrases that end in the middle of sentences and for phrases at the end of sentences.

Narrate a Story Practice Questions

These practice questions will help you prepare to think quickly and respond concisely to *narrate a story* questions. You should take 60 seconds to study each sequence of six pictures before answering the question. Work on one practice question at a time. If you preview all the questions at once, you will ruin the spontaneity. Make your practice as realistic as possible by not looking ahead at other questions and by keeping the time limit. For each set of questions below, record your responses. Then listen to each response to see if you have accurately responded to the specific language function, and if you have appropriately addressed the intended audience. Correct and repeat responses that need improvement.

Practice Question 6.1

Here are six pictures that illustrate a short story. Starting at the beginning, tell me the complete story picture by picture. (60 seconds)

Practice Question 6.2

Here are six pictures that illustrate a short story. Starting at the beginning, tell me the complete story picture by picture. (60 seconds)

Practice Question 6.3

Here are six pictures that illustrate a short story. Starting at the beginning, tell me the complete story picture by picture. (60 seconds)

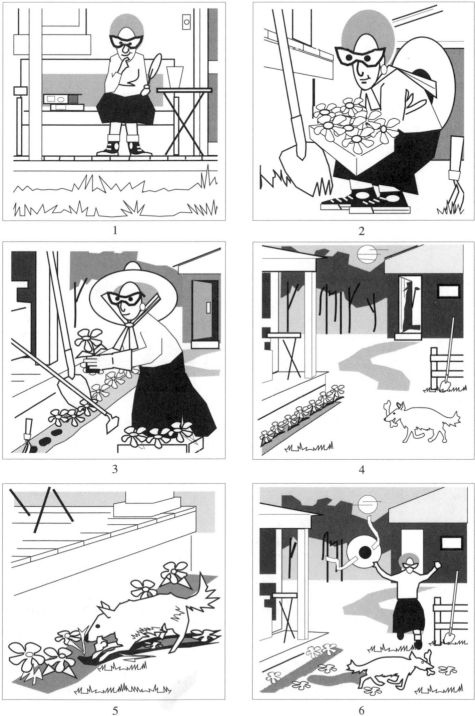

Practice Question 6.4

Here are six pictures that illustrate a short story. Starting at the beginning, tell me the complete story picture by picture. (60 seconds)

1

2

3

4

5

6

Practice Question 6.5

Here are six pictures that illustrate a short story. Starting at the beginning, tell me the complete story picture by picture. (60 seconds)

−7−

Discuss Advantages and Disadvantages

In this chapter you will:

- Become familiar with the instructions for the *discuss advantages and disadvantages* questions of the TSE®.
- See examples of *discuss advantages and disadvantages* questions and corresponding responses.
- Learn what makes an effective response to *discuss advantages and disadvantages* questions.
- Practice responding to a variety of *discuss advantages and disadvantages* questions.

The general directions for the picture section of the test may be something like this:

> **In this section of the test, you will see six pictures that depict a story line. You will be given 60 seconds to review the pictures. After that, you will be asked to tell the short story that is illustrated by the pictures. Try to include all six pictures in your story. When the test narrator tells you to, you may start telling the story.** (preparation time = 60 seconds)

This first test question asks you to narrate the story in the pictures. Communication strategies for narrating a story are described in Chapter 6. The second question generally asks you to discuss the advantages and disadvantages of something that is related to the pictures. Alternatively, you may be asked to compare or to compare *and* contrast issues that are suggested by the pictures.

For the *discuss advantages and disadvantages* question, you may be asked something like this:

> **In the picture sequence you see a person riding a bicycle. Some people get around by using bicycles while other people use cars. Pretend that you are talking to someone who has just arrived in the United States, and tell them about the pros and cons of bicycles and cars as transportation.** (60 seconds)

The topic of the question will usually come from some idea presented in the pictures, but it will extend beyond what is shown in the pictures. Therefore, you have more freedom to use your own ideas in responding to this question. Take a few seconds to think, and then begin your answer with a brief preview. Talk about two or three ideas because time does not allow for more. If the question specifically asks you to talk about two items—in this case, bicycles and cars—then in your answer you should try to cover both items. Be explicit in your discussion of *advantages* and *disadvantages*. While mentioning the advantages of one thing may imply a disadvantage for the other, don't expect raters to make this inference on their own. Be *explicit* about both the advantages and disadvantages you discuss. Then, after talking about both sides of the issue, briefly conclude your answer. Here is an example response:

> *There are both advantages and disadvantages to getting around by either bicycle or car. Two important factors to consider when discussing transportation are cost and convenience. The advantages of owning a bicycle are that you can buy an inexpensive one for about $100 and the cost of maintenance is very low. On the other hand, a reliable car will cost thousands of dollars with hundreds of dollars spent each year on fuel, insurance, and regular mainte-*

> *nance. Convenience is another factor. It is not easy to*
> *travel long distances or in rainy weather on a bicycle, yet*
> *these pose no problem for a car. Furthermore, cars can*
> *carry more luggage than bikes. So if you have enough*
> *money, I recommend that you buy a car to use while you're*
> *in the U.S.*

This response is formal in style. Previewing the ideas to be discussed adds cohesion to the whole response. The first two sentences provide the rater with a clear *preview* of what is to come—that is, a discussion of both the *advantages* and the *disadvantages* of both *bicycles and cars* as forms of transportation. The two specific features to be discussed, *cost* and *convenience*, are highlighted so the rater knows what to listen for.

Each sentence in the body of the response clearly identifies which type of vehicle is being discussed, either bicycles or cars, and which feature is being discussed, either cost or convenience. Details are given to support the statements that are made, such as *you can buy a (bicycle) for about $100 dollars,* and cars have ongoing expenses like *fuel, insurance, and regular maintenance.* Concrete examples communicate your ideas more readily to the rater than do generalizations. For example, rather than saying, "It might be hard for a bicycle to get you somewhere," the response was, *It is not easy to travel long distances or in rainy weather on a bicycle.*

Transitions throughout the response help to make the answer cohesive. The preview statement, *Two important factors . . . ,* was already identified as a cohesive device. *On the other hand, Convenience is another factor, Furthermore,* and *So if you have enough money* are also examples of transitions.

The conclusion is short, just one sentence, but it summarizes the general intent of the response with a recommendation that demonstrates audience awareness by taking into account the listener's situation. This type of conclusion adds cohesion to the response and demonstrates control with the language.

Another possible alternative for responding to this question is more informal in tone and follows:

For living on campus, I think the advantages of owning a bike far outweigh the advantages of owning a car. For one thing, bikes are inexpensive. You can pick up a good bike for about a hundred bucks where a decent car will cost you a couple thousand. Second, there's a problem with parking. It's easy to find a bike rack at all the campus buildings to lock up your bike, but it's impossible to find a parking space for a car unless it's a weekend. You'll want to get a strong lock for your bike too, since every year lots of bikes are stolen. I know that during break you may want to do some traveling, and it would be nice to have a car for that. But don't worry, you can rent a car pretty cheaply, and if you travel with friends you can split the cost. While it may sound nice to own a car, I think you'll be better off getting around campus by bike.

Exercise 7.1: Using Connectors

In this exercise you are given two paragraphs adapted from native speakers' responses. The connector words and phrases have been removed. Read the paragraphs, and decide what connectors go in which blanks. Write the number of the correct connector in each blank.

Paragraph 1

(a)_____, you can go almost anywhere you can see

(b)_____ where you're constrained to riding on the road.

(c)_____ cars do create pollution which make smog and

things which hurts the environment (d)_____ is not good

for people's health. (e)_____ it's a lot easier to ride a car,

you don't have to work as hard. (f)_____ bicycles in general are cheaper in that you only buy them once (g)_____

you don't have to pay for fuel (h)_____ you do with a car.

(i)_____ give you good exercise actually. (j)_____ if I had

to pick I'd probably ride a car (k)_____ I'm a little lazy

(l)_____ bicycles are probably better for the environment.

It just depends on how far you need to go.

1. *alternatively*
2. *like*
3. *even though*
4. *as opposed to a car*
5. *additionally*
6. *and*
7. *and after that*
8. *because*
9. *so overall*
10. *yet I would say*
11. *well as far as bicycles are concerned*
12. *they also*

Paragraph 2

(a)_____ a bicycle is really nice (b)_____ it's very clean.

There's no pollution. It's easy to maintain a bike (c)_____

they're easy to park (d)_____ you don't have to drive

around looking for a parking place. Cars, (e)_____, can go

a lot further. You can drive cars in the winter time when it's

cold outside (f)_____ if it's raining (g)_____ not worry

about the weather. (h)_____, you can fit more people in a

car than you can on a bike. Cars are not that great (i)_____

they have a lot of pollution (j)_____ they're really big

(k)_____ much more expensive.

1. *and*
2. *and*
3. *and*
4. *and*
5. *because*
6. *because first of all*
7. *obviously*
8. *on the other hand*
9. *or*
10. *though because*
11. *well*

Correct grammar is important to communicating clearly. Here is another example response:

> *Uh there there is some advantage and disadvantage using bicycle and car as transportation / if if if / we use bicycle / um / there is a lot of uh / advantage for example is / part of the / physical health / exercise / and also / uh it is more flexible to go / to any place that / very difficult to reaching / using the cars / uh / but there is also the disadvantage of using bicycle / it be time very limited / and also uh / yeah that is not all part of the city you can use eh bicycle / for uh if you use the car / there is some advantage / for example / are the times relatively relative / uh short / to / reach some place / and but there is some disadvantage in the city that / car cannot reach / cannot enter*

Exercise 7.2: Using Correct Grammar

The sentences below were taken from the student response you just read. Rewrite each sentence in correct grammatical form. Say each corrected sentence aloud as fluently as you can.

1. There is some advantage and disadvantage using bicycle and car as transportation.

_____

_____

2. There is a lot of advantage for example is part of the physical health exercise.

_____

_____

3. It is more flexible to go any place that very difficult to reaching using the cars.

_____

_____

4. The disadvantage of using bicycle it be time very limited.

_____

_____

5. Not all part of the city you can use bicycle.

_____

_____

⑤ Exercise 7.3: Brainstorming Advantages and Disadvantages

Practice brainstorming advantages and disadvantages for the topics listed here. These topics are good classroom discussion topics but are unlikely to be used on the test. Time yourself, and allow one minute for each topic. The first one has been done for you.

Topic	Advantages	Disadvantages
1. Electronic publishing and Web journals	World-wide accessibility Easy to search articles Saves cost of printing and mailing Quicker publishing time	Not accessible without a computer and network connection Easier to plagiarize Uncertainty of how long articles will be available on-line Dependent on technology Personal cost to print out articles
2. Cloning		
3. Standardized testing		
4. Income tax		
5. Employee drug testing		
6. Bilingual education		

⑤ Exercise 7.4: Discussing Advantages and Disadvantages

Choose one of the topics from Exercise 7.3. Time yourself for one minute, and discuss the advantages and disadvantages of the topic. If you can work with a partner, ask him or her for some feedback on your communication ability. If you do not have a partner to work with, record your response and analyze it yourself.

●→ Tips for DISCUSSING ADVANTAGES AND DISADVANTAGES QUESTIONS

1. Begin your response by identifying the issues you will be discussing.
2. Clearly identify comments as either an *advantage or disadvantage*. Do not assume that listeners will infer this for themselves.
3. Use *concrete examples* to illustrate your points.
4. Use *transition words and phrases* when moving from one point to the next.
5. If you finish slightly before the minute is over, don't force yourself to say more if you have nothing more to add.
6. Don't worry if you didn't complete your discussion of advantages and disadvantages. The raters will rate the language sample you did provide.
7. Let both the words and the tone in your voice express the importance or value of the issues discussed.
8. Pause in grammatical places. Link the sounds within any single phrase. Include primary stress on each phrase, and alternate pitch between stressed and unstressed syllables. Use appropriate intonation for phrases that end in the middle of sentences and for phrases at the end of sentences.

Discuss Advantages and Disadvantages
Practice Questions

These practice questions will help you prepare to think quickly and respond concisely to *discuss advantages and disadvantages* questions. Work on one practice set at a time. If you preview all the questions at once, you will ruin the spontaneity. Make your practice as realistic as possible by not looking ahead at other questions and by keeping to the time limit. For each practice question, record your response. Then listen to each response to see if you have accurately responded to the specific language function and if you have appropriately addressed the intended audience. Correct and repeat responses that need improvement.

Practice Question 7.1

A variety of foods are served at most restaurants. Some people like to eat meat in their diet, but others like to eat only vegetables. Pretend you are talking to a few of your colleagues and tell them the pros and cons of both types of diets. (60 seconds)

Practice Question 7.2

The person in this picture sequence is shown with a car. Some people purchase cars, and others decide to lease them. Pretend you are talking to a colleague, and explain the pros and cons of purchasing versus leasing a car. (60 seconds)

1

2

3

4

5

6

Practice Question 7.3

This picture sequence includes a dog. Some people like to have pets. Pretend you are talking to a colleague, and tell your colleague about the pros and cons of owning a pet. (60 seconds)

Practice Question 7.4

Some families are large, and others are small. Pretend that we are neighbors and tell me about the pros and cons of being the oldest child in a family versus being the youngest child in a family. (60 seconds)

Practice Question 7.5

Many homes have television sets, but not everyone thinks watching television is good. Pretend you are talking with a colleague, and explain to your colleague the pros and cons of having or not having a television set in your home. (60 seconds)

Share an Opinion

In this chapter you will:

- Become familiar with the instructions for the *share an opinion* questions of the TSE®.
- See examples of *share an opinion* questions and corresponding responses.
- Learn what makes an effective response to *share an opinion* questions.
- Practice responding to a variety of *share an opinion* questions.

The general directions for this section of the test may be something like this:

The next few questions will ask you about your thoughts on a number of different issues. Think for a couple of seconds before you begin answering. Try to answer as thoroughly as you can in the time given for each question.

The questions in this section can cover a wide range of topics, but no special expertise is expected on your part. This chapter covers the *share an opinion* type questions, and Chapter 9 covers the *discuss a hypothetical situation* questions. In order to accomplish these communication goals in the small amount of time given to respond, you will need a strategy and some practice. The raters don't expect you to begin speaking immediately, so don't start speaking your response immediately after the question is given. Take a few seconds to organize your thoughts.

For the *share an opinion* question, you may be asked something like this:

> **Many large cities like Baltimore, Chicago, and Seattle have aquariums where people can view sea animals. However, some people think that sea animals should not be taken out of nature and forced to live in small aquarium tanks. Please tell me your opinion about this question.**
> (60 seconds)

After the question is given you should quickly decide on the opinion you will defend. It is not important for the purpose of the test which side of the issue you take. Choose the side that is easiest for you to talk about and explain. Maybe in your heart you don't believe in aquariums, but it's hard for you to explain why you believe this in concrete, rational terms in English. If you know concrete reasons for keeping aquariums, and it is easier for you to express these reasons in English, then go ahead and choose this side to defend. Here is an example response:

> *I believe society should keep aquariums. Two important reasons for keeping aquariums are for research and public awareness. First of all research done on sea animals at aquariums benefits sea animals in the wild. If humans are serious about helping sea animals live in the wild, we must do all we can to learn about sea animals through research both in the wild and in aquariums. Second, aquariums help to keep people interested in sea animals and aware of the growing number of endangered species. Children especially like aquariums, and if children grow up with a love for sea animals, they will be more likely to*

> *make sacrifices to help make sure natural habitat is set*
> *aside for sea animals. So while some people think that*
> *aquariums are a bad place for individual sea animals to*
> *live, it is really the best way to help sea animal popula-*
> *tions live better lives in our world.*

This response is formal in style. The language function of this question is sharing an opinion, which is composed of giving an opinion and defending that opinion. In this response, the opinion is given at the beginning and accomplishes the function of giving an opinion. That is a good way to begin since it lets the rater know exactly what side is being defended. The second sentence gives a clear preview of the two main ideas to be discussed, *research* and *public awareness.*

The language function of defending an opinion is accomplished in the body of the response. In defending an opinion, it is important to consider the arguments of the other side. Someone opposed to aquariums is likely to say that aquariums take away freedom from sea animals, and sea animals may be unhappy or unhealthy in aquariums. To head off these types of counterarguments, the response shows that sea animals in aquariums help sea animals in the wild through the knowledge gained by research and the support gained through public awareness.

Cohesion is maintained with a transition to the body of the answer, *First of all.* The next main idea is also introduced with a transition, *Second.* The last sentence provides a summary of the answer, more sea animals are helped by keeping a few of them in aquariums. A clear summary leaves the rater with a strong impression that this response has accomplished the language functions of giving and defending an opinion.

Here is another possible response to this question that supports the opposite view in a coherent manner.

> *Aquariums are definitely degrading to ocean animals.*
> *Both the size of the tanks and their forced dependence on*
> *man show disrespect for these majestic forms of wildlife.*

> *Living space is of primary concern. Take whales, for example, no matter how big you build the tank, it will never be deep enough or wide enough to give the whale the freedom it deserves. Second is the forced dependence on humans that ocean animals experience when held in captivity. The shark is a good example. Sharks were designed as hunters; when they are forced to give up hunting, as they are in aquariums, they lose their natural identities.*
>
> *Although aquariums are popular, I never visit them because it breaks my heart to see these wonderful ocean animals in small tanks and forced to eat at the bidding of their keepers.*

Here is an example response to this same question:

> *mmm I thin(k) I agree with the idea of / not having animals / in small places in those big cities / I thin(k) / (pause) / there should be another way that you can / at least make people enjoy / those animals but / to make / at least big animals / live in those small places / yust (just) for the enjoying of the people / it's a little bit cruel so / I don't agree with the idea of having those aquariums in those city / even though they keep their natural / as better as they want but / as they / they can but / in your case I don't like that idea*
> (10 seconds remaining)

This speaker states his opinion that he does not like aquariums for large animals because he says it is cruel. He anticipates the counterarguments that people enjoy aquariums and that the natural settings in aquariums can be very nice, which shows good audience awareness. The opinion is stated twice with slightly different forms. In the beginning the opinion is stated as *I agree with the idea of not having animals,* and in the middle it is restated as

I don't agree with the idea of having those aquariums. While each statement is correct and consistent with the other, it may be confusing for the listener to hear the same opinion in different formats. There are some minor pronunciation errors at the sound level, such as the missing *k* on *think* and a *y* sound instead of a *j* sound on *just.* The speaker does a good job of placing phrase stress on *not, small,* and *big* in the first two lines. Some problems with grammar in the last two lines may leave a bad impression on the listeners. *Those city* could be revised to *those cities,* and *they keep their natural as better as they want* could be revised to *they make the aquarium environments as natural as possible,* and *in your case* could be revised to *in this case.*

Here is another example response:

> *I think uh / this way is / good / even though we have to pay*
> *the price that taking some anim(al) out of nature / as*
> *pointed out in the paragraph / however I think this price is*
> *worth it / because it allows / it provides / uh more chances*
> *for people to have / to / uh / learn animals / and maybe*
> *learn to love animals / aft / after all not all people have*
> *chance to go outside / and uh / to / uh / get in touch with*
> *some animals / and uh / some animals maybe / uh only live*
> *in some / uh / some other states / some other countries /*
> *and uh without this means we / we don't have any chance*
> *to / uh / to / to learn what's the animal is / at all / and uh /*
> *so overall I think this is good*

In this response the speaker does a good job of placing phrase stress. For example, in the expression *learn animals, learn* was given phrase stress instead of the last word in the phrase, *animals,* to better contrast with *love animals,* where *love* received stress. For clarity, the expression *for people to have to learn animals* could be revised to *for people to learn about animals.* This speaker tends to hesitate at the start of many phrases by restating words or using filler sounds, such as: *it allows-it provides; aft-after all; and uh to uh get; some uh some other states; we-we don't have; to uh to-to learn.* If you have a similar problem, try taking a breath before starting new phrases.

⑤ Exercise 8.1: Speaking Fluently

In this exercise the student response has been rewritten without the repetitions and fillers. Read each line. Then look up and say each phrase as fluently as you can. Don't worry if you don't remember the words exactly as long as you convey the general meaning. Your focus should be on speaking in reasonable message units without hesitations or fillers.

1. I think aquariums are good even if we have to pay the price of taking some animals out of nature.

2. However, I think this price is worth it because it provides a chance for people to learn about animals and maybe learn to love animals.

3. After all, not all people have the chance to get outside and get in touch with animals.

4. Some animals may only live in another state or country.

5. Without aquariums we may never get to learn about those animals.

An example response from a native speaker of English is provided.

> *I think that / to an extent / um / it's ok to take sea animals out of the sea and put them in tanks / uh / the reason this is good is because it really helps to educate the public / about / um / these animals / how they live / and / um it just helps people learn about them / appreciate them / uh and understand them better / on the other hand sometimes these animals are not very well taken care of / um / in that case it would probably be better for them to stay / in the sea / another problem is / that / sometimes the animals might get sick / uh when they're*

> *in captivity / uh / (cough) / so / in that case / it might be*
> *better to let the animals go / occasionally there are ani-*
> *mals that are endangered and*

Notice that even this native speaker uses some filler sounds like *um* and *uh* and even coughs toward the end. The filler sounds do not become overly distracting for this speaker because she was able to maintain a smooth flow of sounds within message units and a good rhythm overall. The speaker also uses a number of words and phrases to link the content into a coherent whole; some example phrases include: *I think that; the reason this is good is because; on the other hand sometimes; in that case; another problem is;* and *so in that case.* Rather than making sweeping generalizations that may be hard to believe, the speaker qualifies her statements with expressions like: *to an extent; sometimes; probably; sometimes; might get sick; it might be better;* and *occasionally.* This speaker seemed to add the phrase *to an extent* as an after-thought or side comment. As such she chose to drop her pitch rather than jump her pitch on the phrase stress. Rise-to-mid-range intonation was used after the phrase stress.

⑤ Exercise 8.2: Practicing English Rhythm

To accurately produce English rhythm in your speaking, it is important to use unstressed vowel sounds for unstressed sylla-bles. If full or stressed sounds are used, then unstressed sylla-bles may sound stressed and interfere with the rhythm. In the previous example response, the native speaker used an un-stressed sound for unstressed vowels. An example of this is the word to. *The vowel sound is pronounced* uh *and is sometimes given the symbol* ə, *which is labeled schwa. In the following phrases, try to use the schwa sound, pronounced* uh, *for the word* to. *Avoid using a rounded /o/ sound as you might for the words* new *or* blue.

1. to take sea animals

2. to educate the public

3. to stay in the sea

4. to let the animals go

The schwa sound may be used for unstressed syllables within stressed words. For example, the i *in* animals *can be pronounced with the unstressed schwa sound.*

Exercise 8.3: Brainstorming Reasons for Your Opinion

When you share your opinion, it is important to state the reasons for your opinion. Now take some time to practice thinking of reasons quickly. Time yourself for a total of five minutes, and list at least three reasons under each of the five statements below.

1. Commuters in urban areas should be required to carpool.

_____

_____

_____

2. A college education should be mandatory.

_____

_____

_____

3. A course in ethics should be required for all college degrees.

_____

_____

_____

4. Doctors should deliver babies in the mother's home.

_____

_____

_____

5. The federal government should provide a free computer to every home.

_____

_____

_____

Now choose one of the topics and present the given argument with the reasons you have listed to a partner. Ask your partner to evaluate how well you organize your reasons, transition between reasons, and open and close your argument. If you do not have a partner to work with, record your response and analyze it yourself.

►→ Tips for SHARE AN OPINION QUESTIONS

1. Take a few seconds to think about your response before speaking, so you can begin with a strong start.
2. Do not worry about trying to give an opinion that will please the rater or that is popular or politically correct. Rather, choose an opinion that allows you to express your own ideas easily.
3. Begin your response by clearly stating your opinion on the given topic.
4. Provide reasons for your opinion that are clearly explained with concrete examples.
5. If you have time, show audience awareness by considering opposing views and explaining why your opinion is better.
6. If you finish slightly before the minute is over, don't force yourself to say more if you have nothing more to add.
7. Don't worry if you don't finish before the time is up. The raters will rate the language sample you did provide.
8. Let both words and the tone in your voice emphasize your opinion and supporting points.
9. Pause in grammatical places. Link the sounds within any single phrase. Include primary stress on each phrase, and alternate pitch between stressed and unstressed syllables. Use appropriate intonation for phrases that end in the middle of sentences and for phrases at the end of sentences.

Share an Opinion Practice Questions

These practice questions will help you prepare to think quickly and respond concisely to *share an opinion* questions. Work on one practice question at a time. If you preview all the questions at once, you will ruin the spontaneity. Make your practice as realistic as possible by not looking ahead at other questions and by keeping the time limit. For each set of the following practice questions, tape-record your responses. As you listen to your recorded responses, check if you have clearly stated and defended your opinion. Also listen to how coherent and fluent your response sounds. Correct and repeat responses that need improvement.

Practice Question 8.1

Some people enjoy living in large urban areas. Other people prefer living in rural areas. Please tell me where you'd prefer to live and why. (60 seconds)

Practice Question 8.2

Due to budget cuts, some schools have to limit some of their programs. Some believe art courses, band, and orchestra should be eliminated. Others say physical education and sports teams should be cut. What is your opinion? Which programs do you think schools should cut, and why? (60 seconds)

Practice Question 8.3

Some people have suggested that the United States should not use pennies for currency anymore. Other people disagree. Please tell me what you think about this issue. (60 seconds)

Practice Question 8.4

Some people think that the government should provide health care for all citizens. Other people think that citizens should be responsible for their own health care. Please tell me your opinion about this topic. (60 seconds)

Practice Question 8.5

Some parents like to know the gender of their baby before it is born. Other parents prefer not knowing the gender until after it is born. Please tell me your opinion about this topic. (60 seconds)

Practice Question 8.6

New medicines take many years to get from the research lab to the market-place due to strict government regulations. Some people think the government regulations should be loosened in order to get needed drugs to the public quicker. Please tell me your opinion about this topic. (60 seconds)

Practice Question 8.7

It is often difficult to get doctors to practice medicine in rural areas. Some people believe the government should provide bonuses to doctors who work in rural areas. Please tell me your opinion about this topic. (60 seconds)

Practice Question 8.8

Doctors typically pay large premiums for medical malpractice insurance, which results in an overall increase in the cost of health care. Some people think there should be caps on the lawsuits brought against doctors to help control insurance costs. Please tell me your opinion about this topic. (60 seconds)

Practice Question 8.9

Some people think a common monetary unit across countries, like the euro, will be good for the economy, while others feel it will hurt the economy. Please tell me your opinion about this topic. (60 seconds)

Practice Question 8.10

Many technology jobs have been relocated from the United States to locations where the cost of living and the price of labor are less expensive. Please tell me your opinion about this topic. (60 seconds)

–9–

Discuss a Hypothetical Situation

In this chapter you will:

- Become familiar with the instructions for the *discuss a hypothetical situation* questions of the TSE®.
- See examples of *discuss a hypothetical situation* questions and corresponding responses.
- Learn what makes an effective response to *discuss a hypothetical situation* questions.
- Practice responding to a variety of *discuss a hypothetical situation* questions.

The general directions for this section of the test may be something like this:

> **The next few questions will ask you about your thoughts on a number of different issues. Think for a couple of seconds before you begin answering. Try to answer as thoroughly as you can in the time given for each question.**

The questions in this section can cover a wide range of topics but no special expertise is expected on your part. Chapter 8 covered the *share an opinion* type questions, and this chapter covers the *discuss a hypothetical situation* questions. A hypothetical situation is a situation that is imaginary, though it could be true in the future. Hypothetical situations allow you to be creative with your answer since you are not restricted by describing what actually is real. On the other hand, don't create a hypothetical situation that is so unreal that it is unbelievable or confusing. As with the previous question, take a few seconds to organize your thoughts.

For the *discuss a hypothetical situation* question, you may be asked something like this:

> **If you were given a million dollars to donate to one charity, what charity or type of charity would you give it to?** (60 seconds)

There are hundreds of potential charities you could donate to. Don't let the freedom to choose interfere with providing a good response. Don't waste a lot of time thinking of the absolute best charity or comparing between charities to determine which one is most important to you. Since you can speak about any charity, choose one that you know or care about so that it will be easy for you to talk about. If you don't know anything about cancer research or charities for cancer research, don't choose this charity just because you believe it is the most important. It might be easier to talk about donating money to the hospital or library in your home town. While that hospital or library may not make it onto a worldwide charity list, it might be a good choice if you can explain how important that hospital or library is to the community and how an increase in funds could improve services.

The key to responding is to clearly identify the charity or type of charity and to explain why this might be a good choice. Here is an example response:

> *There are a LOT of good charities out there / if I had a million dollars / I think I would give it to MEDICAL research / research is needed for CANCER / for MS / and / uh / ALZHEIMER'S disease / uh / ok / let's say I donate the money to CANCER research / almost EVERYONE knows*

> *SOMEONE **who's been affected by cancer** / there's SKIN*
> *cancer / COLON cancer / BREAST cancer / PROSTATE*
> *cancer / (pause) / **and many** OTHER **types of cancers** /*
> ***research has helped advance early** DETECTION **of many***
> ***forms of cancer** / **but if cancer is** TRULY **to be controlled** /*
> ***then some form of cancer** PREVENTION **must be devel-***
> ***oped** / **With** LESS **government money for education and***
> ***research** / **money from** OTHER **sources** / **is needed to keep***
> ***the research** GOING / **I'd be** VERY **happy** / **if the money I***
> ***donated lead to a significant discovery** / **that helped pre-***
> ***vent or cure** CANCER / **It's a** BIG **job though and will take***
> ***the work of a lot of** . . .*

This response starts by saying there are a lot of *good charities*, then narrows the focus to *medical research*, and finally focuses on *cancer research*. It's as if the speaker were talking through his choice of topics. While this strategy works for this speaker, he may want to think for a few seconds before beginning and just start by saying something like, *I think cancer research is a worthy charity to donate to.* Another strength of this response is the phrase stress, which has been highlighted in capital letters. In the list of cancers, rather than stress the word *cancer* each time, the speaker places stress on each type of cancer (skin, colon, breast, prostate, other). To convey the hypothetical nature of the donation, the speaker uses the expressions *I would* and *I'd.* The word choice accurately and concisely conveys the speaker's meaning with words such as: *detection, prevention, controlled, developed,* and *significant.* The tone is conversational with expressions like: *a lot of, I think I would, very happy,* and *a big job.* The use of contractions also adds a casual sound: *let's, who's, there's, I'd,* and *it's.* The words and stress show enthusiasm for making a difference with this hypothetical donation. Although the speaker is cut off from completing his last sentence, his score will not be lowered because of this since he has adequately addressed the question.

In the example response that follows, look for how the hypothetical nature of the response is expressed.

I think / for a million dollars I would give it to some type of medical research like cancer / um / this is a disease that / affects almost everyone and / being able to find medicines or treatments or even a cure for this / uh would just be a real benefit to society / (cough) um / other types of medical research are also good / uh to donate money to but cancer is one where I just feel like / so many people are affected by it / um / that that would be a good place for the money to go (20 seconds remaining)

In this response, underline the word *would* each time it is used. *May, might,* and *would* are important words in conveying hypothetical information.

🔊 Exercise 9.1: Discussing the Future

Complete the following information. With a partner discuss the future you anticipate for your home country. Remember, the words may, might, *and* could *are useful in discussing future possibilities.*

Name of home country: _____

_____

Approximate population: _____

_____

Type of government: _____

_____

Natural resources: _____

_____

Industries: _____

_____

Here are some example sentences:

- *My country might be able to expand in international trade.*
- *Wood is an abundant natural resource, and if we can develop the furniture industry, we might be able to make better use of it.*
- *If our population continues expanding at the current rate, we could be facing a food shortage within 20 years.*

Here is another example response:

> **I think / I will / uh / give uh / my money / to / charities uh which / help people in / Africa / I saw a lot of country (ies) / in that / in those cit / in those countries vely (very) poor and / they don't have enough food to eat / the people there / looks vely (very) thin and / unhealthy / so I think if I have / a lot of money / I will give them / some money to help them / because um / we are all human / we should all help each other** (15 seconds remaining)

This response does a good job of identifying a type of charity, *help people in Africa*. It also provides a rationale for helping others even if we don't know them because *we are all human*. The opening could be strengthened by thinking for a few seconds before speaking and clearly stating the charity without hesitations, such as: *I think I would give my money to help hungry people in Africa.* The speaker responds with hesitancy and effort indicated by repetitions like: *in that, in those cit, in those countries.* The speaker mentions that the people are thin and unhealthy. The time remaining at the end of the response suggests that the speaker could go into more detail. She could mention some of the causes of hunger, such as wars and drought. This speaker has some trouble with /r/ sounds as indicated in the word *very*. If the speaker is aware of this problem she could practice words that contain *r* that she frequently uses in order to pronounce them more accurately.

---

⑤ Exercise 9.2: Practicing Pronunciation of R and L

The letter r *can appear at the beginning, middle, or end of words. It can appear connected to a vowel or consonant. Some people have difficulty when the letters* r *and* l *appear in the same word.* L *is pronounced with the tip of the tongue touching the tooth ridge.* R *is pronounced by curling back the tongue without letting the tongue touch the roof of the mouth. Here are some terms from the University Word List to practice your pronunciation of* l *and* r. *Say each word aloud, repeating it as necessary to get it pronounced correctly. Record yourself or ask someone for feedback. Create a sentence for each word for more contextualized practice. The first three sentences have been created for you.*

1. *accelerate*

   If we accelerate our reading schedule, we can spend more time on the research projects at the end of the semester.

2. *alternative*

   You have two alternatives for this project: summarize a journal article on this topic or conduct an interview and summarize it.

3. *circulate*

   While you do your experiments I will circulate through the lab to help with any problems.

4. *clarify*

_____

_____

5. *internal*

_____

_____

6. *interval*

_____

_____

7. *journal*

_____

_____

8. *laboratory*

_____

_____

9. *lecture*

_____

_____

10. *material*

_____

_____

11. *neutral*

_____

_____

12. *overlap*

_____

_____

13. *perpendicular*

_____

_____

14. *preliminary*

_____

_____

15. *principle*

_____

_____

16. *rational*

_____

_____

17. *relevance*

_____

_____

18. *similar*

_____

_____

19. *surplus*

_____

_____

20. *terminology*

_____

_____

21. *tolerate*

_____

_____

Your words:

22. _____

_____

_____

23. _____

_____

_____

24. _____

_____

_____

25. _____

_____

_____

Here is another example response:

> *Mm / ha for me it's a little bit easier (laugh) this question /*
> *I will geeve (give) all the mowney (money) to a third*
> *world sharity (charity) / I leef shor fildren (I feel for chil-*
> *dren) in / in those / countries / because I SAW how they*
> *suffer / I SAW the powverty (poverty) / I SAW the situation*
> *that they can LIVE / oh / under / the situation under / they /*
> *try to develop their skills / and then they try to live / and /*
> *ah it's awful so / I will give my ENTIRE money / just / for*
> *those children in those countries / this will make the*
> *future a little bit better* (10 seconds remaining)

As with the other sample responses, a specific charity was not named, but a type of charity was clearly identified: children in third world countries. Communication is compromised due to pronunciation problems with vowels and consonants. In the first couple of lines there are a number of problem areas. The *i* in *give* is pronounced like a long *e* rather than a short *i*. The *o* in *money* is pronounced as a rounded *ow* rather than an unrounded mid-mouth sound. The consonant /ch/ is confused with /sh/ in *charity*, and the /f/ and /l/ sounds are reversed in *feel*. The /ch/ and /f/ sounds are reversed in the words *for* and *children*, and /sh/ is substituted for /ch/. A wider mouth position is needed for pronouncing the *o* in *poverty*. Phrase stress is placed on the verb *saw* all three times it is used. Perhaps this emphasizes that the speaker personally witnessed this suffering. However, he may want to place phrase stress on *suffer, poverty,* and *situation* to emphasize the children's experience more than his own. The speaker uses the word *so* to indicate a summary statement at the end. The summary statement provides a brief wrap-up statement for this response.

🔊 Exercise 9.3: Giving a Hypothetical Response

For each situation pretend you are a university instructor and respond appropriately. Give your response aloud to a partner or record and listen to your responses. Check your accuracy of the use of may, might, *and* would. *The first response has been done for you as an example.*

1. A student asks you a question you don't know the answer to. What would you do?

   <u>If I got a question I didn't know the answer to, I would</u>
   <u>admit I didn't know. I might also ask if there was anyone in</u>
   <u>the class that did know the answer. If it was a problem to</u>
   <u>solve, I might explain the approach I would use to try and</u>
   <u>solve that problem.</u>

2. Your students look bored. What would you do?

   _____

   _____

   _____

3. The projector goes out, and you have no way to show your power point slides. What would you do?

   _____

   _____

   _____

4. You forget your lesson plan in your office. What would you do?

   _____

   _____

   _____

5. Pretend you are a teacher and your students complain that you haven't graded their exams yet. What would you do?

_____

_____

_____

6. Pretend another instructor asks to observe you. What would you do?

_____

_____

_____

7. Pretend your office mate plays the radio too loud. What would you do?

_____

_____

_____

8. Pretend you have five minutes left of class with 15 more minutes of material to cover. What would you do?

_____

_____

_____

➡ Tips for DISCUSS A HYPOTHETICAL SITUATION QUESTIONS

1. Take a few seconds to think about your response before speaking, so you can begin with a strong start.
2. Do not worry about making the best choice. Choose something you feel comfortable talking about.
3. Begin your discussion by clearly identifying your choice in the given hypothetical situation.
4. Explain the reasons for your choice. Use concrete details to illustrate what you mean. You may use personal experience to make your discussion more vivid.
5. If you finish slightly before the minute is over, don't force yourself to say more if you have nothing more to add.
6. Don't worry if you don't finish before the time is up. The raters will rate the language sample you did provide.
7. If you know certain English sounds are difficult for you to pronounce, practice saying words you use frequently that contain these sounds.
8. Let both words and the tone in your voice emphasize your main points.
9. Pause in grammatical places. Link the sounds within any single phrase. Include primary stress on each phrase, and alternate pitch between stressed and unstressed syllables. Use appropriate intonation for phrases that end in the middle of sentences and for phrases at the end of sentences.

Discuss a Hypothetical Situation
Practice Questions

These practice questions will help you prepare to think quickly and respond concisely to *discuss a hypothetical situation* questions. Work on one practice question at a time. If you preview all the questions at once, you will ruin the spontaneity. Make your practice as realistic as possible by not looking ahead at other questions and by keeping the time limit. For each set of practice questions that follow, record your responses. As you listen to your recorded responses, check if you have discussed the situation in enough detail for someone else to understand. Also listen to how coherent and fluent your response sounds. Correct and repeat responses that need improvement.

Practice Question 9.1

If you were able to decide the criteria for an all-expenses-paid college scholarship, what criteria would you choose? (60 seconds)

Practice Question 9.2

If you could choose to have dinner with any famous living person in the world, who would you choose? (60 seconds)

Practice Question 9.3

If you could be the author of any kind of book, what kind of book would you choose to write? (60 seconds)

Practice Question 9.4

If you could learn another language besides English, what would you choose? (60 seconds)

Practice Question 9.5

If you could start a new business, what kind of business would you start? (60 seconds)

Practice Question 9.6

If you could live anywhere in the world, where would you choose to live? (60 seconds)

Practice Question 9.7

If you could choose to be any kind of doctor, what kind of doctor would you choose to be? (60 seconds)

Practice Question 9.8

If you were invited to give a commencement address at your university, what topic would you choose to speak on? (60 seconds)

Practice Question 9.9

If you could go anywhere on sabbatical, where would you choose to go? (60 seconds)

Practice Question 9.10

If you could attend any professional conference, which conference would you choose to attend? (60 seconds)

–10–

Describe a Graph

> In this chapter you will:
>
> - Become familiar with the instructions for the *describe a graph* questions of the TSE®.
> - See examples of *describe a graph* questions and corresponding responses.
> - Learn what makes an effective response to *describe a graph* questions.
> - Practice responding to a variety of *describe a graph* questions.

The general directions for the graph section of the test may be something like this:

> **Here is a graph of State University's enrollment over two decades. You now have 15 seconds to review the graph.**
> (preparation time = 15 seconds)

In this example the graph is about enrollment at State University. The general directions will focus on identifying the title or some basic characteristics of the graph that is provided. While everything in the general directions may be learned from the graph itself, these details in the general directions should help you quickly focus on the important features of the graph. This chapter covers the *describe a graph* questions, and Chapter 11 covers the *analyze a graph* questions. Use the 15 seconds to study the graph to gain a solid understanding of the information it contains. Identify the variables and the units of measure. See if there are any noticeable trends over time. The graph may take a number of forms such as two sets of bars on a bar graph, two pie charts side by side, or two lines on a graph. Look for ways the information compares and contrasts.

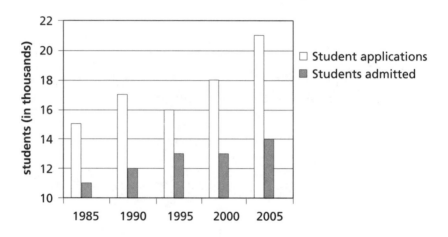

Enrollment for State University

When the 15 seconds to review the graph are over, you may be asked something like this:

> **Please tell me about the information portrayed in this graph.** (60 seconds)

In describing the graph, focus on the content of the graph. While it may help to explain some of the graphical features of the graph, such as what the shading means or the variables on the horizontal and vertical axes, it is more important to demonstrate that you have the ability to put the meaning of the data into words. Reading the labels on the axes and the legend may sound mechanical and unnatural. Most graphs have numbers. Don't worry about reading the numbers on the graph to a high precision. It is better to quickly approximate. Some speakers don't mention the numbers at all; instead they focus on the trends and comparisons. An example response to this question is:

> *This graph portrays um / student enrollment and applicat /*
> *or students actually admitted and their applications /*
> *(clears throat) / to this university / as a function of year /*
> *um / there's some interesting / things that are going on*
> *here you can see there is a uh / a dip in applications in*
> *nineteen ninety five / whereas in general there is an upward*
> *trend / um / from eighty five to two thousand five so in*
> *ninety five the number of applications dropped / uh / even*
> *though the number of applications was large um / the*
> *number of people- students actually admitted / was*
> *relatively low / on the order of a half to a third / um /*
> *interestingly in nineteen ninety five when / the applications*
> *dropped / um there is a higher percentage of people*
> *admitted so / the admiss- the admissions / while they did*
> *increase a little bit / year to year / didn't go up nearly as*
> *much as the applications went up /*

The speaker gives a strong opening statement with the phrase, *this graph portrays*. Other useful expressions to begin describing a graph include:

- *This graph portrays, shows, illustrates, depicts . . .*
- *The title of this graph is . . .*

The speaker identifies two critical variables under comparison in the graph: *enrollment* and *applications*. Specific vocabulary is used to get the speaker's ideas across. For example, the expression *as a function of year* is a mathematical or scientific way to describe a graph that represents data over time. Alternative expressions include:

- *applications and enrollment according to year . . .*
- *applications and enrollment by year . . .*
- *applications and enrollment every five years between 1985 and 2005 . . .*

The speaker never mentions the specific number of applications or students enrolled. Rather, he describes the graph in general with phrases like: *a dip in applications, in general there is an upward trend, the number of applications dropped, was relatively low, on the order of a half to a third, a higher percentage, increase a little bit,* and *didn't go up nearly as much.* With this strategy the speaker avoids bumbling over numbers or losing his audience by mechanically reciting the numbers for each bar on the graph for each year. The result is that the speaker is able to convey the overall meaning of the graph quickly.

Even though there are some hesitations (*um*) and some rephrasing (*the admiss- the admissions*), message units are spoken fluently with linked sounds and accurate word and phrase stress. Overall, this would be considered a strong response.

In the next example response, the speaker is able to describe the overall content of the graph and also includes some specific numbers from the graph.

> ***This graph compares the number of student applicants to the number of students admitted uh / over a period of twenty years in five-year increments / and it looks like / uh there are always more students who apply than are actually / admitted / and applica- applications increase / um every five years except for nineteen ninety five / also / the number of students admitted increases / except for the year two thousand when the number admitted stays level at around thirteen thousand students / the increase in students admitted over this twenty year period isn't nearly as much as the increase in applications / by two thousand and five / State University is receiving approximately uh / twenty one thousand applications / but admitting only fourteen thousand students***

As in the previous example, a strong opening statement is made by high-lighting the comparison between applicants and students admitted. The time frame is expressed in a sophisticated manner by stating: *over a period of twenty years in five-year increments.* Early in the response the data is described in general terms: *more students who apply than are actually admitted.* The speaker also points out exceptions to the trends: *applications increase every five years except for 1995.* Toward the end of the response the speaker starts giving some numbers: *thirteen thousand, twenty one thousand,* and *fourteen thousand.* These numbers are qualified with expressions like: *around* and *approximately.* Cohesion is maintained in the comparison described in the response with these expressions: *this graph compares, more students who apply than are, isn't nearly as much,* and *but admitting.* Intonation and phrase stress also enhances cohesion. Contrasting stress is used on the words *applicants* and a*dmitted* in the phrase *the number of student applicants to the number of students admitted.* Low-range intonation is used consistently at the ends of sentences, and rise-to-mid-range is used for mid-sentence phrases.

---

⑤ Exercise 10.1: Speaking Fluently

The following sentences were adapted from the previous example response. Determine where you would pause for message units and where you would place phrase stress for each message unit. Say each sentence aloud as fluently as you can. The first one has been marked for you.

1. This graph compares the number of student **APP**licants / to the number of students ad**MI**tted / over a period of twenty **YEARS** / in five-year **IN**crements.

2. It looks like there are always more students who apply than are actually admitted.

3. Applications increase every five years except for nineteen ninety five.

4. Also the number of students admitted increases except for the year two thousand when the number admitted stays level at around thirteen thousand students.

5. The increase in students admitted over this twenty-year period isn't nearly as much as the increase in applications.

6. By two thousand and five State University is receiving approximately twenty-one thousand applications but admitting only fourteen thousand students.

Here is another example response:

> *The type of this graph / is the enrollment of State University / um / the x-axis provide(s) us the years / such as nineteen eighty five / nineteen ninety / until two thousand and two / and the y-axis / uh provide (s) us the information / that how many students / applied / or admitted to this university / uh from this graph we can see that from nineteen eighty five / to ninety / to two thousand five / both the / eh eh / students / applicated to this university / or admitted to this university / increased / uh especially / for the / for those students appl / ap- apply to this university / in nineteen eighty five / it was / uh / fifteen thousand / however in nine / two thousand two / it wa / it is . . .*

This speaker begins with the title of the graph and then describes the x and y axes. To get across the point that the time scale is in five-year increments, the speaker starts listing the years. With each year in the list, good rise-to-mid-range intonation is used until the end of the sentence when down intonation is used. This last year is mistakenly called 2002 instead of 2005. There are no penalties for small errors in reading the graph. Later in the response the year is correctly stated as 2005, and in the last line it is mistakenly referred to as 2002 again. In this case there is no data for 2002, so it is clear that the speaker is talking about 2005. However, if there were data for each year and 2005 were mistakenly referred to as 2002, then this would be confusing to the listener and may detract from the score.

The speaker points out the general trend that both the number of *applications* and students admitted has increased. It is unclear what the speaker intends to point out by highlighting 1985 with *especially*. Applications exceed admittances for each year listed and the number of applications in 1985 is not a maximum, so it is unclear what is special about 1985. There are a few other phrases that are not as precise as they could be. The phrase *the type of this graph* could be reworded to *the title of this graph*. The phrase *both the students applicated to this university or admitted to this university* could be reworded to *both the students who applied to this university and those who were admitted to this university*. In this sentence *applied* is the correct word form, and the word *and* conveys the idea of both better than the word *or*. The overall organization of this response is acceptable, but the delivery would limit its communicative effectiveness.

Here is another example response:

> *From the graph we can see the students' / applications / uh . . . / begin / began in nineteen eighty five in number of about fifteen thousand / and / and in / two thousand and five about / twenty one thousand / and at the same time the students admitted by the univ / by the State University / beginning in / nineteen fifty eight / the number was / about / eleven thousand / and two / two thousand and five / it reached fourteen thousand / and we can see the / for the trend of the student applications / eh / the gradual tendency / is / upgoing but / uh from / nineteen ninety to nineteen ninety five there is a kind of long going / and uh / and for the situation of students admitted . . .*

This speaker jumps into a detailed description of the graph by stating the number of applications in 1985 and 2005, and then stating the number of students admitted in 1985 and 2005. Discourse organization might be improved by starting with an overview such as: *This graph provides data on the number of applications and admittances from 1985 to 2005 at State University.* Toward the end of the response some overall comments about the graph are shared, such as: *for the trend of* and *the gradual tendency.* Phrases like *upgoing* and *long going* give a sense of the meaning but may be confusing to the listener. *Upgoing* may be rephrased as *increasing,* and *long going* may be rephrased as *slight decrease.* Certain expressions are common when describing graphs and when used properly may help to improve your fluency when discussing a graph. Some of these graph expressions are listed in the chart.

Lines	Areas	Trends	Changes
solid line	shaded area	increase	rapid
dashed line	dotted area	decrease	slow
dotted line	blackened area	rise	sudden
straight line	cross-hatched area	fall	gradual
curved line	checkered area	decline	moderate
horizontal line		drop	exponential
vertical line		jump	consistent
		leveling off	
		plateau	

⑤ Exercise 10.2: Describing a Graph

Look at the following graph. Using words from the chart, write five sentences that describe the graph. Say each of your sentences aloud. Ask a partner or an ESL instructor for feedback on your language use and how you sound. Alternatively, record yourself saying the sentences and give yourself feedback. After practicing your sentences, practice describing the graph in a coherent manner. An example description has been done for you.

Households with Internet in 1995

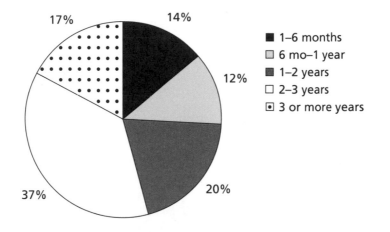

17% 14%

12%

■ 1–6 months
□ 6 mo–1 year
■ 1–2 years
□ 2–3 years
⊙ 3 or more years

37% 20%

Households with Internet in 2000

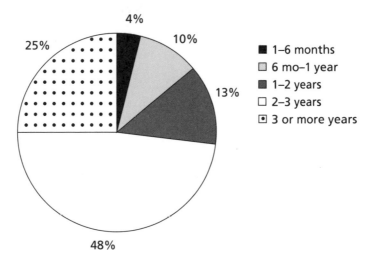

4%

25% 10%

13%

■ 1–6 months
□ 6 mo–1 year
■ 1–2 years
□ 2–3 years
⊙ 3 or more years

48%

1. <u>The cross-hatched area shows that the percentage of households with Internet connections for more than three years has increased rapidly from 1995 to 2000.</u>

2. _____

_____

3. _____

_____

4. _____

_____

5. _____

_____

6. _____

_____

⑤ Exercise 10.3: Recording a Description of a Graph

Find a graph in a newspaper, magazine, or book. Many newspapers like USA Today *and the* Wall Street Journal *are good sources for graphs. Record yourself describing the graph for one minute. Assess how well you gave the overall meaning of the information, highlighted comparisons and contrasts, and pointed out any special features of the graph.*

Here is another example response to the State University graph.

> *In this graph / we can see / from nineteen eighty five to two*
> *thousand and five / there is a um / a increase-in(g) train*
> *(trend) / of students applicants / and also there is a goo /*
> *uh / train (trend) of a / of a increasing trend of students*
> *admitted in the university / but / in / the students admitted*
> *in the university is relatively s / small / compared to the*
> *students' applicants (applications) / so / and but / so um /*
> *in / as a general / the students admit in the university was /*
> *was increasing and al / that shows that / this is a good*
> *trend for the society as / m-many peoples go to universities /*
> *that will / they can im / improve their uh knowledge / and*
> *they can do better to the society / they can contribute what*
> *they learn / in / a school / and / but who / for a student*
> *who / applicants they / they don't um get admitted to the*
> *socie / to colleges / they can also learn a lot um / same*
> *knowledge from other area like from work . . .*

The first half of this response focuses on describing the State University graph. After a brief overview of the graph, the speaker goes on to analyze it. There is no penalty for analyzing as well as describing, but with only 60 seconds to respond, it might be better to focus on the main task of describing. Focusing on the task of describing allows you to develop a clear explanation, including comparing and contrasting the data shown in the graph. The question following the *describe a graph* question is typically an *analyze the graph* question. If you analyze the graph during the time to describe the graph, you may not have anything more to say for the *analyze a graph* question, or you may not feel comfortable repeating some of the things you just said.

➞   Tips for DESCRIBE A GRAPH QUESTIONS

1. Begin describing the graph by stating the title.
2. Identify the important variables.
3. Give an overview of the data by explaining overall trends or generalizations.
4. As time allows, describe the details of the graph.
5. If comparative data are shown, explain some of the ways the data compare and contrast.
6. Explain any special symbols used in the graph.
7. Avoid losing time by trying to read the numbers on the graph too accurately. Round numbers, and qualify with expressions such as *about* and *approximately.*
8. If time allows, summarize the main point of the graph at the end.
9. If you finish slightly before the minute is over, don't force yourself to say more if you have nothing more to add.
10. Don't worry if you didn't finish describing the graph. The raters will rate the language sample you did provide.
11. Let both the words and the tone in your voice emphasize key points and comparisons and contrasts.
12. Pause in grammatical places. Link the sounds within any single phrase. Include primary stress on each phrase and alternate pitch between stressed and unstressed syllables. Use appropriate intonation for phrases that end in the middle of sentences and for phrases at the end of sentences.

Describe a Graph Practice Questions

These practice questions will help you prepare to think quickly and respond concisely to *describe the graph* type questions. You should take 15 seconds to study the graph before describing it. Work on one practice question at a time. If you preview all the questions at once, you will ruin the spontaneity. Make your practice as realistic as possible by not looking ahead at other questions and by keeping the time limit, 15 seconds to preview the graph and 60 seconds to describe it. For each set of questions, record your responses. Then listen to each response to see if you have accurately described the overall meaning of the graph and highlighted any key comparisons or contrasts. Correct and repeat responses that need improvement.

Practice Question 10.1

Please tell me about the information portrayed in this graph. (60 seconds)

Average Household Budget in 1995

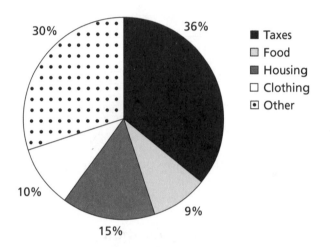

Average Household Budget in 2000

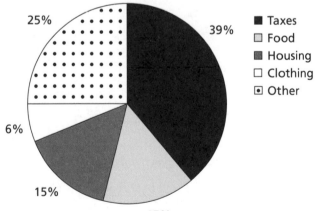

Practice Question 10.2

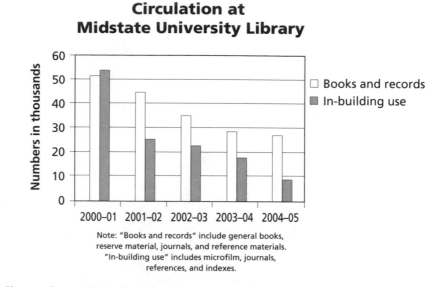

Circulation at Midstate University Library

Note: "Books and records" include general books, reserve material, journals, and reference materials. "In-building use" includes microfilm, journals, references, and indexes.

Please tell me about the information portrayed in this graph. (60 seconds)

Practice Question 10.3

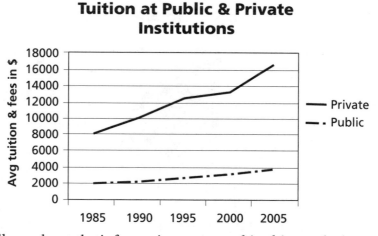

Tuition at Public & Private Institutions

Please tell me about the information portrayed in this graph. (60 seconds)

Practice Question 10.4

Unemployment Rates

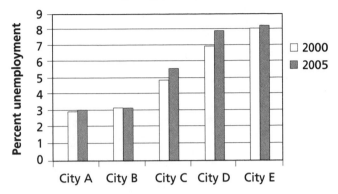

Please tell me about the information portrayed in this graph. (60 seconds)

Practice Question 10.5

Exercise Characterisitics in Counties

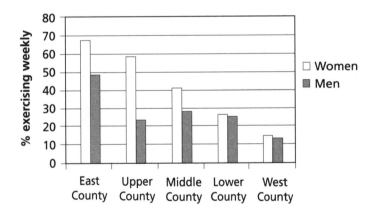

Please tell me about the information portrayed in this graph. (60 seconds)

Practice Question 10.6

Farming Trends

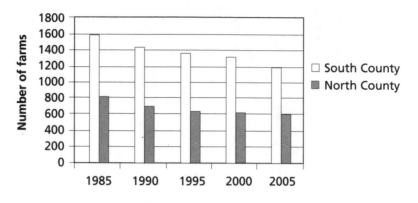

Please tell me about the information portrayed in this graph. (60 seconds)

–11–

Analyze a Graph

In this chapter you will:

- Become familiar with the instructions for the *analyze a graph* questions of the TSE®.
- See examples of *analyze a graph* questions and corresponding responses.
- Learn what makes an effective response to *analyze a graph* questions.
- Practice responding to a variety of *analyze a graph* questions.

The general directions for the graph section of the test may be something like this:

Here is a graph of State University's enrollment over two decades. You now have 15 seconds to review the graph.
(preparation time = 15 seconds)

In this example the graph is about enrollment at State University. Chapter 10 covers the *describe a graph* questions, and this chapter covers the *analyze a graph* questions. After studying the graph for 15 seconds and describing it for 60 seconds, you should have a fairly good understanding of what it shows. In the *analyze a graph* question, do not merely continue describing the graph as shown. You will be expected to *discuss possible reasons for the information.* You might not know the full background on the graph, and there may be many possible explanations for the information. It is not important whether you have the correct analysis or the best analysis. The question is given to assess your ability to communicate your own analysis of graphical data. Since you only have 60 seconds to respond, do not get stuck in an explanation of an overly complex analysis. Think of reasons that are straightforward and concrete. This will allow you to focus on language and communication rather than difficult content.

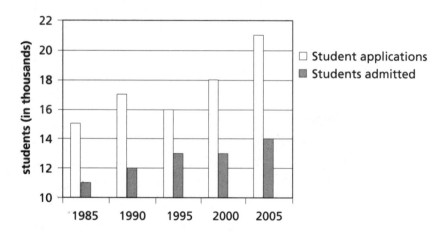

Enrollment for State University

After being asked to describe the graph, you may be asked something like this:

Please propose some reasons that may explain the data shown in the graph. (60 seconds)

Some people get nervous trying to respond to this type of question because a logical reason may not come to mind immediately. One way to prepare is to think about *categories or themes* that often cause changes, such as economics, politics, technology, education, and culture and values. For a given issue, try to think which category provides the most logical reasons for the information. Generally it is better to focus on one reason, or maybe two, and to provide supporting details.

⑤ Exercise 11.1: Using Categories to Explain Scenarios

Following each scenario is a list of categories. Write a reason after each category that could potentially explain the scenario. The first one has been done for you.

1. A change in students' test scores could be attributed to:

Economics: An increased school budget allowed hiring of more teachers and smaller classes to provide more individualized attention.

Politics: An implementation of standardized testing from the local authorities helped eliminate differences in grading.

Technology: Computers provided students easy access to more information.

Education: The changes in teaching methods encouraged deeper learning.

Culture and values: If a culture values education at well-known institutions then students may be influenced to strive to do better on tests in hopes of entering a quality school.

Note: Without knowing more background information, we can't be sure which, if any, of these reasons is correct. But any one of them could be developed into a coherent response.

2. A reduction in the number of nurses could be attributed to:

Economics: _____

_____

Politics: _____

_____

Technology: _____

_____

Education: _____

_____

Culture and values: _____

_____

3. A reduction in the cost of medications could be attributed to:

Economics: _____

_____

Politics: _____

_____

Technology: _____

_____

Education: _____

_____

Culture and values: _____

_____

4. An increase in the number of construction injuries could
   be attributed to:

   Economics: _____

   _____

   Politics: _____

   _____

   Technology: _____

   _____

   Education: _____

   _____

   Culture and values: _____

   _____

5. An increase in the number of visa requests could be
   attributed to:

   Economics: _____

   _____

   Politics: _____

   _____

   Technology: _____

   _____

   Education: _____

   _____

   Culture and values: _____

   _____

Now go back and choose one scenario for which you will give a 60-second response. Do not describe all potential reasons as listed; rather, choose one reason and explain it in detail. Share your answer with a partner. Your partner can provide feedback on how coherent your response is. If you do not have a partner to work with, record your response and evaluate it yourself. Rephrase confusing sentences and then try recording a second time.

Here is an example response based on the graph for Enrollment at State University:

> ***mm that's a tougher one uh / I think the uh / one thing uh / (cough) if actual applications went down / as in nineteen ninety five / that could be maybe the economy was going really well that year and uh / you know that will um / that will impact maybe less people thought they needed / more education because they already had a job / um / other than nineteen ninety five / there is a general trend upward for applications received / which could mean that / uh more people wanted to go to college / which probably meant that either the job situation or the um / careers that they wanted required an education / as more and more people realized this uh / and the school's actual admissions went up probably because they were increasing capacity / hiring more teachers or / uh building more classrooms and things like that***

The graph shows data for student applications and student admissions, and the response provides reasons for the changes seen in both. Economic and education reasons are suggested for the changes in applications. If the economy is strong and people readily find good work without more educa-tion, then there is less economic motivation to apply to a university. If education becomes a necessary prerequisite for more and more jobs, then people have more motivation to apply to a university. Reasons for changes in students admitted are related to resource allocation, such as *hiring more teachers* and *building more classrooms.*

At the beginning of this response the speaker is thinking aloud. He comments that this question is harder than the previous one (*mm that's a tougher one uh*). He hesitates a couple of times before he starts his analysis: *I think the uh / one thing uh / (cough) if.* This speaker sounds very natural as though he is comfortably talking with a friend about what he is thinking. However, some people do not sound natural when they do not have a clear direction for what they want to say. For those kinds of speakers it is often helpful to take a few seconds to quietly gather some thoughts before speaking and then start with a strong opening statement that previews the main ideas. For example, this speaker could have said, *Economics and education are the most probable causes for changes in the number of student applications while resource allocation may influence the number of students admitted.* To add extra emphasis to key ideas, there could be a short pause after the words *economics, education,* and *resource allocation.* A brief pause after key words helps the listeners to process these key words and categorize them as significant.

Since the speaker can't be absolutely positive if his reasons are accurate or not, he uses phrases like: *if actual applications, maybe the economy, maybe less people, which could mean, which probably meant, probably because,* and *things like that.* All of these indicate the speaker is expressing possibilities rather than verifiable conclusions. This speaker stays on task, speaks with clear pronunciation, and conveys his ideas in a coherent manner. Despite the hesitations, this would be considered a moderately strong response.

Ⓢ Exercise 11.2: Speaking Fluently

In this exercise the student response has been rewritten more concisely. Read each line. Then look up and say each phrase as fluently as you can. Don't worry if you don't remember the words exactly as long as you convey the general meaning. Your focus should be on speaking fluently, with reasonable message units and correct phrase stress.

1. Actual applications went down in nineteen ninety five.

2. Maybe the economy was going really well that year.

3. So maybe less people thought they needed more education because they already had a job.

4. Other than nineteen ninety five, there is a general trend upward for applications received.

5. This probably meant that either the job situation or the careers that they wanted required an education.

6. The school's actual admissions went up probably because they were increasing capacity by hiring more teachers or building more classrooms.

Here is another example response:

Cause if we look back into / the history you can see / maybe twenty years ago the / uh / it's the / i i i it's the start of the growing birth rate of the county / so for each year you will find more / and more coming / new students / and they will apply for university / so that's why the students' application / is growing / uh / and uh / and meanwhile of course / the university accepts more and more fund(s) from the government / and also / some donations from some / alumni / so the students could be ad / admitted by the university is also increasing / uh / however / there is a kind of / uh / down / just a going down trend from nineteen . . .

Although this response is less sophisticated than the previous one, it still shows good coherence. It provides reasons for the growing number of applications and the growing number of students admitted. The speaker uses his imagination and suggests that the students come mainly from one county and that this county had an increase in birth rate starting 20 years ago. At the end, the response begins to address the dip in applications in 1995, but time runs out. This response is a little short even though the speaker was talking the whole time. This indicates some lack of fluency. The score may be reduced for lack of fluency, but it would not be reduced for being cut off or not finishing the response.

⑤ Exercise 11.3: Rewording for Clarity

Some of the phrases in the previous response could be reworded for clarity. Suggest clear alternative expressions for each phrase that fit the context of the response. The first one has been done for you.

1. *into the history*

   <u>into the history behind the graph</u>

2. *more and more coming new students*

   _____

3. *apply for university*

   _____

4. *students' application is growing*

   _____

5. *so the students could be admitted by the university is also increasing*

   _____

6. *there is a kind of just a going down trend*

   _____

Here is another example response:

> *From the graph we know that uh / the number of / the*
> *student who / are admitted / from / State University is / is*
> *much lower / than the number of student who apply for*
> *the university / so I think a / a university should uh /*
> *should help uh / admit more students so that they can /*
> *attend the State University otherwise they have to go to*
> *private one / that mean they need to pay more for the*
> *tuition* (15 seconds remaining)

In the first half of this response the speaker describes the graph again. In the second half she shares her opinion about why State University should accept more students. No reasons for the data are suggested. Therefore, this response would be scored low. Additionally, many of the message units have a flat tone, and the response is very short with time remaining.

Here is another example response:

> *hm / some of the reason can be / (laugh) this university / I*
> *don't know (spoken softly) / found new / departments that*
> *ə need / more people / there was a greater investment dur-*
> *ing the year nineteen (eighty five) to ninety five so / there*
> *was more places for ə students in their university / and / as*
> *you can see here the / students admit during those years*
> *was almost the same from nineteen ninety five to two*
> *thousand five / so maybe their reputation of the university*
> *increased during those year / so the number of application*
> *increased / but the university just can / admit / the same*
> *amount of / student / a certain amount of student that /*
> *was the same the results ten years / mm /*

The speaker suggests that new departments were created at the university, which increased enrollment. He also proposes that the university's reputation increased and prompted more students to apply. The task of analyzing the graph was accomplished, but the communication was inhibited by pronunciation and grammar. An extra *uh* sound, symbolized by ə, was placed between words in these phrases: *that ə need* and *for ə students*. This added vowel sound distorts the rhythm and makes it difficult for listeners to process the information. This happens most often between adjacent consonants within words and between words. If you hear yourself with this problem, you can create a smoother link between the sounds by holding back some air when pronouncing the first consonant. Added vowel sounds also happen with some speakers before words starting in *s* when the *s* is followed by another consonant, as in the words *students* and *school.*

⑤ Exercise 11.4: Creating a Smooth Link between Sounds

Each of the sentences describes the value of questioning in the classroom. Underline all adjacent consonants and words beginning with an s *plus a consonant. Say each sentence aloud as one message unit. Focus on linking consonants together, and pronouncing words beginning with* s- *plus a consonant without adding extra vowel sounds. The first sentence has been underlined for you.*

1. Que<u>stio</u>ns can <u>st</u>imulate <u>st</u>ude<u>nt</u> i<u>nt</u>ere<u>st</u> in a topic.

2. Asking questions is a good strategy to encourage communication between the instructor and students.

3. Questions help to focus the attention of students on important points.

4. Questions provide an opportunity for students to struggle with content to obtain deeper learning.

5. Student skill and confidence are developed as they learn to respond to questions.

6. Questions give students practice in structuring ideas and speaking clearly.

7. Questions prompt students to think through sticky issues for themselves.

8. Questions and the struggle to answer them can build group cooperation in the classroom.

9. The instructor can take steps to assess the scope of learning through student responses to carefully crafted questions.

⑤ Exercise 11.5: Speaking Grammatically

The sentences in this exercise were taken from the response on page 148. Rewrite each sentence in correct grammatical form. Reword for brevity and clarity as needed. Say each corrected sentence aloud as fluently as you can.

1. Some of the reason can be this university found new departments that need more people.

   _____

   _____

2. There was a greater investment during the year 1985 to '95 so there was more places for students in their university.

   _____

   _____

3. As you can see here the students admit during those years was almost the same from 1995 to 2005.

_____

_____

4. So maybe their reputation of the university increased during those year.

_____

_____

5. So the number of application increased but the university just can admit the same amount of student, a certain amount of student, that was the same the results ten years.

_____

_____

Here is another example response:

> *Well it looks like over time / uh more students are interested in attending college / um / the college also appears to be growing / probably um / overtime people realized that / to get better jobs they're going to need a little bit better education / and / (clears throat) so more people are wanting to attend college / and the colleges are also admitting more people / uh / to prepare the / population for the workplace / it could also be that other universities nearby have closed / or significantly raised their tuition / so / State University would look more attractive to more students / Why isn't State University growing more? / well / it might be because there are not enough state funds to expand quicker / these are just a few possible reasons that applications have increase so much / and students admitted have increase only a little bit / . . .*

This response analyzes both the large rise in the number of student applications and the small rise in the number of students admitted. To say this much with 60 seconds the speaker had to be very fluent in English. Still there are some hesitations like *well* or *um*, but these are used in a natural way and do not interfere with communication. The rhetorical question, *Why isn't State University growing more?* is used effectively, and the conclusion briefly summarizes the key ideas. Phrase stress and intonation are used accurately throughout. This would be considered a strong response.

●→ Tips for ANALYZING A GRAPH QUESTIONS

1. Do not repeat a description of the graph. Focus on the specific analysis questions asked like discussing possible reasons that explain the data in the graph.

2. Remember categories of causes to help you think of reasons that explain the information in the graph, such as economics, politics, technology, education, and culture and values.

3. Focus on one, maybe two causes, and explain those in detail. Do not list a half dozen causes without explaining any one of them very well.

4. Think before you begin speaking, and start with a fluent sentence that previews the main ideas.

5. If time allows, summarize the main point of the analysis at the end.

6. If you finish slightly before the minute is over, don't force yourself to say more if you have nothing more to add.

7. Don't worry if you didn't finish analyzing the graph. The raters will rate the language sample you did provide.

8. Let both words and the tone in your voice emphasize key points and logical connections.

9. Pause after key words or phrases to provide time for listeners to process what you are saying.

10. Pause in grammatical places. Link the sounds within any single phrase. Include primary stress on each phrase, and alternate pitch between stressed and unstressed syllables. Use appropriate intonation for phrases that end in the middle of sentences and for phrases at the end of sentences.

Analyze a Graph Practice Questions

These practice questions will help you prepare to think quickly and respond concisely to *analyze a graph* questions. You should study the graph in each practice question before analyzing it. Work on one practice question at a time. If you preview all the questions at once, you will ruin the spontaneity. Make your practice as realistic as possible by not looking ahead at other questions and by keeping the time limit. For each set of questions, record your responses. Then listen to each response to see if you have clearly explained your analysis of the information in the graph in a fluent manner. Correct and repeat responses that need improvement.

Practice Question 11.1

Average Household Budget in 1995

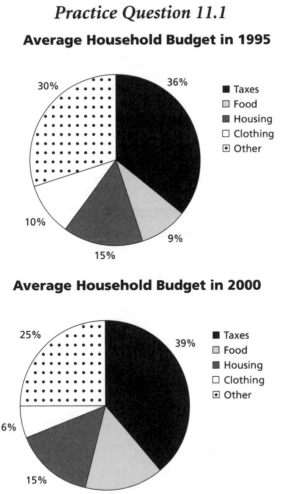

Average Household Budget in 2000

Please propose some reasons that may explain the data shown in the graph. (60 seconds)

Practice Question 11.2

Circulation at Midstate University Library

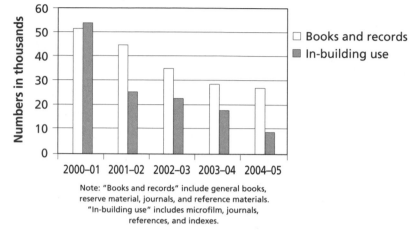

Note: "Books and records" include general books, reserve material, journals, and reference materials. "In-building use" includes microfilm, journals, references, and indexes.

Please propose some reasons that may explain the data shown in the graph. (60 seconds)

Practice Question 11.3

Tuition at Public & Private Institutions

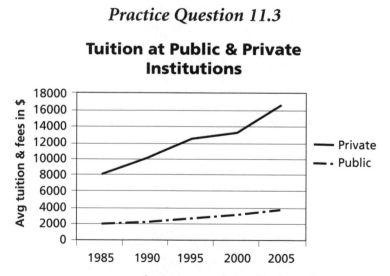

Please propose some reasons that may explain the data shown in the graph. (60 seconds)

Practice Question 11.4

Unemployment Rates

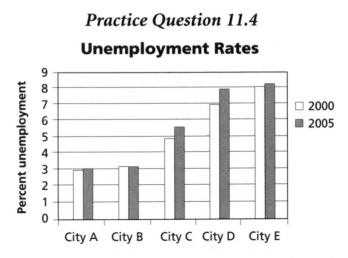

Please propose some reasons that may explain the data shown in the graph.
(60 seconds)

Practice Question 11.5

Exercise Characterisitics in Counties

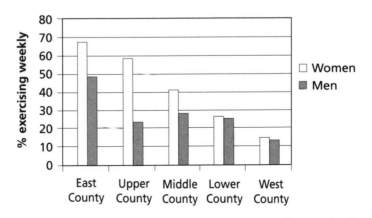

Please propose some reasons that may explain the data shown in the graph.
(60 seconds)

Practice Question 11.6

Farming Trends

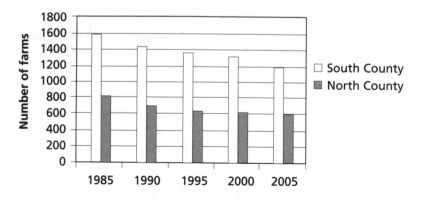

Please propose some reasons that may explain the data shown in the graph.
(60 seconds)

–12–

Extend a Greeting

In this chapter you will:

- Become familiar with the instructions for the *extend a greeting* questions of the TSE®.
- See examples of *extend a greeting* questions and corresponding responses.
- Learn what makes an effective response to *extend a greeting* questions.
- Practice responding to a variety of *extend a greeting* questions.

The general directions for the *extend a greeting*, the *respond to a phone message*, and the *give a progress report* questions may be something like this:

For the next three questions, you are to pretend that you work in a business setting or are talking with someone about business. These situations provide you with an opportunity to demonstrate how well you can converse in a business environment. Your response should be suitable for addressing the people and context provided in the situation of each question. You may find it helpful to take notes as you listen.

This question tries to provide some kind of context for you to demonstrate the appropriateness of your language, or your sociolinguistic competence. The context will most likely be a business, commercial, or industrial setting, although it could be an academic or social setting as well. The relationship of the person you pretend to talk with will be defined in the question, such as business colleague, unknown company representative, work supervisor, new acquaintance, peer, or friend.

The *respond to a phone message* questions and the *give a progress report* questions are the only questions with listening passages, so this is the first time in the test where you are encouraged to take notes. You are free to take notes during any portion of the test, but you may find it most helpful for the questions with listening passages. If you do take notes it is best to write key words or short phrases and then to briefly order these for your response. Don't try to write out everything you want to say; you won't have time. Use the notes to trigger your memory so that you can focus on speaking fluently. If taking notes distracts you, do not take notes.

The *extend a greeting* question may be something like this:

In this situation you will be asked to talk with a business associate. Pretend that your business associate has just recently started his or her own business. Greet your business associate and be sure to:

- **say something about the new business,**
- **say something positive regarding the new business, and**
- **offer appropriate wishes to the business associate.**

Use the next 30 seconds to prepare your response. I will indicate when you should begin speaking. (preparation time = 30 seconds)

You may begin your response now. (60 seconds)

Although there is no preparation time for this question, you may think for a few seconds before speaking. The question provides an outline for your response:

- greet the colleague,
- mention the business,
- react positively, and
- extend appropriate wishes.

Try to include all four aspects in your response, so be careful not to spend too much time on any one aspect. Since the type of business is not mentioned, you should feel free to choose one. Pick something you feel comfortable talking about. For example, if you know a lot about sports, you might congratulate your colleague on opening a sports equipment store, or if you love fine coffees, you can pretend your colleague has opened a coffee house. If you don't know anything about computers or construction, you won't want to pretend that your colleague has started an on-line business or a construction company. It is generally easier to talk about topics that are familiar to you.

Let's take a look at one example response to this question.

Hi / Peter / people told me that you just opened a coffee shop / across / the street of Psychology Building / isn't it true? / Wow! / Congratulations! / I guess you should have a lot of customers / going to your / coffee shop / I know that there is no coffee shop around the Psychology Building / there should be / um / so you should have a lot of customers / oh do you have um / wireless Internet in your coffee shop? / I know that a lot of people / um like to go to the coffee shop with the lap top / so if you / um / if you installed wireless Internet in your coffee shop / then a lot of people would go to your coffee shop / and that's really attractive / I think / so if you haven't installed a wireless Internet I suggest you to do so / maybe / it can attract more customers / ok um / I wish you / um / good luck with your / new

> *business / and I'll see you around your new coffee shop / I*
> *will uh / find some time to go to your coffee shop to have a*
> */ cup of coffee / bye bye /*

This response was delivered well and addresses all parts of the task. It begins with a simple but effective greeting *Hi Peter* and is followed by mentioning the new business. The name Peter and the business of a coffee shop were invented by the speaker and give her something concrete to talk about. This also makes the response more realistic. The positive reaction is clearly communicated with words like *wow* and *congratulations.* In addition to these well-chosen words, the positive reaction is communicated with intonation that expresses excitement, indicated in the text with exclamation marks. At the end of the conversation, the speaker tells the business associate *good luck* and mentions that she will *go to your coffee shop to have a cup of coffee.*

In addition to addressing the four parts asked in the question, this speaker also mentions the location and expresses why she thinks this is a good location for a new business. She also asks the business associate whether or not the coffee shop has a wireless Internet connection. These additional items go beyond the task and help the one-sided conversation to keep flowing; however, it is not necessary to go beyond the task in order to perform well on this question.

Now that we've discussed the content of the message, let's talk about the linguistic features. In general, the speaker pauses in appropriate places to make grammatically meaningful phrases or message units. However, during the greeting, the speaker pauses between *Hi* and the name *Peter* when it would sound better to say the two words together. The pause between *going to your* and *coffee shop* could be eliminated as well. Many of the phrases are quite long and show advanced fluency by linking words together for a smooth flow of sound and by using rhythm appropriate for English. For a phrase like *people told me that you just opened a coffee shop,* a less fluent speaker might feel more comfortable pausing after *people told me.* Either one long phrase or two short phrases is acceptable; however, it would not be acceptable to pause after every or almost every word.

There are some pauses for filler words like *um, uh,* and *ok.* Even native speakers will use filler sounds. If these are short in duration and infrequent, they do not interrupt the flow of the conversation. Frequent use of filler sounds, such as after every other phrase, can become distracting. Most phrases have one strong stress or primary stress along with a good alternation of pitch on stressed and unstressed syllables to create appropriate rhythm. However, the intonation on *I know that there is no coffee shop around the Psychology Building* sounded flat. It might help the speaker to pause after *shop*. During the test, some examinees find it helpful to move their hand forward, point their finger, or nod their head as they speak to remind them to alternate pitch or to emphasize primary stress.

This speaker also used appropriate intonation on questions, such as the tag question, *isn't it true?* and the yes-no question, *do you have wireless Internet in your coffee shop?* Since the intonation dropped after the primary stress, the tag indicates that the speaker is fairly confident that what she just said is indeed true. If high-range intonation were used, then it would indicate that the speaker was uncertain as to how true the last statement was. For the yes-no question the speaker used high-range intonation after the primary stress; however, a low-range intonation would be equally acceptable. On the phrase *I guess you should have a lot of customers,* the speaker used low-range intonation. Since this phrase is not the end of a sentence, rise-to-mid-range intonation would be the correct way to signal to the listener that more information is coming.

This speaker sounds very natural with her greeting (*Hi Peter*), her congratulations (*Wow! Congratulations!*), and phrases like *I guess you, oh do you have,* and *I think.* Yet some of the wording seems a bit formal. The phrase *people told me* could be changed to *I heard* or *someone told me.* The negative form of the tag question *isn't it true?* sounds more formal than *is it true?* The general singular *with a lap top* or the plural *with lap tops* is preferable to the specific *with the lap top.* Lap top acts as a compound noun and the speaker correctly placed stronger stress on *lap*. The phrase *that's really attractive* sounds a little stiff. It could be reworded as *that would attract a lot of people* or *that would be really popular.* The phrase *I suggest you to do so* could be reworded as *I suggest that you do it* or *I recommend that you give it a try.*

There is no one right way to respond to the type of question where you are asked to greet someone and wish them well on their current activities. Some additional example responses follow.

> *Hi Bill / uh it's good to see you here / uh I heard that you /*
> *just started a / new coffee house this town / few days ago /*
> *and / I actually visited your coffee house yesterday / uh / I*
> *was impressed by the interior design / and I thought / the*
> *location is great / and / the most important / uh the flavor*
> *of the coffee was fantastic / I really enjoyed it / us so / uh / I*
> *hope / your coffee house will draw a lot of people / and / I*
> *am quite sure / that uh people will / uh keep coming to*
> *your coffee house once they visit / your coffee house / uh /*
> *good lick on your business!*

This speaker accomplishes the four tasks involved in the question. Accurate intonation patterns are used. Mid-sentence phrases carry rise-to-mid-range intonation (*design* and *great*), and ends of sentences carry low-range intonation (*fantastic* and *enjoyed it*). The frequent use of filler sounds tends to be distracting though.

Here is another example response:

> *Hi Mi(ke) / congratulation(s) / on your new business? /*
> *(did) you / start up / a business on / peer-to-peer search*
> *engine company? / that's a great idear / now / peer-to-peer*
> *system / are / more and more popular / lots of people using /*
> *peer-to-peer / system to search / dentistry (industry) /*
> *movies / _____ shows / but / we / we need / a good*
> *techenolgy (technology) to help research / those stuff / and*
> *there / there / there isn't / the good product for help in*
> *these (this) / market / so your business / will open a new*
> *business (line of business) / on this market / (which) is*
> *really a great idear / and I wish you / success / and help*
> *(hope) you / beat Google / to be / come (become) the*
> *number one / peer to peer / circling (searching) system*

This speaker gave a greeting based on a creative technology company. All four parts of the questions are included in the response; however, the response is weakened by missing sounds and words as noted in the parentheses. Rising intonation is used correctly on the yes-no question *search engine company?* but is used incorrectly on the congratulatory statement *on your new business.* An /r/ sound has been added to the word *idea.* This happens after a vowel when the tongue is raised too high in the mouth. An extra sound has been added to the word *technology* between the *ch* and the *n.* Some speakers have trouble linking adjacent consonant sounds without adding a vowel between. Some words are difficult to distinguish, such as *dentistry* for *industry* and *circling* for *searching.* While the core of this response is good, the delivery could be improved.

⑤ Exercise 12.1: Marking Intonation

Before each phrase indicate what type of intonation would be appropriate by marking: **H** *for high range;* **L** *for low range;* **RM** *for rise-to-mid-range. Say each phrase aloud with the appropriate intonation.*

Response A

_____ 1. Hi,

_____ 2. how are you doing?

_____ 3. I heard you're starting a new business.

_____ 4. That's really exciting.

_____ 5. How are things going with that?

_____ 6. Tell me a little bit about your business.

_____ 7. Things sound really good.

_____ 8. I wish you really great luck

_____ 9. and success with that.

_____ 10. I hope that things turn out really well for you.

Response B

_____ 1. Hello,

_____ 2. how are you?

_____ 3. I got word that you are starting a software
business.

_____ 4. I'm very happy that I have a friend

_____ 5. who wants to try to develop a business.

_____ 6. I hope you can compete with the big
companies

_____ 7. because competition improves the market.

_____ 8. More companies mean

_____ 9. better quality

_____10. and better prices.

Exercise 12.2: Practicing Intonation

*Greet three people today and compliment them. You can talk
with people you know, like a friend or colleague, or someone
you don't know, like a bus driver or store clerk. Practice proper
intonation as you speak.*

⑤ Exercise 12.3: Analyzing Extend a Greeting Responses

Look at the sample responses in this exercise. Identify strengths and weaknesses of each response. The first one has been started for you.

Hi Mary / I knew that you just set up a new restaurant on Green Street / is that true? / yeah / I think that's SO great / you know / there are so many students at the university / and most of the students / you know / will go out for / lunch / because they do not have enough time to prepare their lunch / so that I think your restaurant will have a / a lot of / customer(s) / and if your restaurant is a GOOD restaurant / that / is uh / in a style of uh / Asian food / I think MORE students / including Asian / and westerners / will go these / uh do you have a good cook now? / oh / you hired a good cook from Chicago? / that's even greater / I think a cook / a good cooker / is uh / half of the success of the restaurant / and I know that / you have a / good management / capabilities / so I / I'm sure that your restaurant will earn a lot of money / and / I do wish that / you will get more success / get / more money in your own business / and I hope that I can go to your restaurant for a free meal / ok? / bye

Strengths	Weaknesses
pronunciation Good stress (So, More, Good)	*pronunciation*
wording Appropriate greeting (Hi Mary)	*wording* I knew that you just set up could be changed to I heard that you just set up
coherence / organization	*coherence / organization*
other	*other*

> *Hi John / I heard that you opened a new restaurant on Green Street / congratulation / I think that's a good idear / to open the lestaruant / on Green Street because there is / no other / restaurant / on GREEN Street / so / uh / to be a good rest / aurant / I'd / like suggest / two thing / for you / uh first one / keep your restaurant clean / so / if you / uh if the restaurant is dirty / it / can give the customer / bad*

> *impression so they / not / gonna visit again / so that the one*
> *good point for / good restaurant and / the other one is / uh /*
> *make variety of food / menu / uh so it can give customer /*
> *have a multiple choice to eat / so that's another things / so*
> *I hope / uh your restaurant gonna be one of famous*
> *restaurant / in this town / and good luck to your business*

Strengths	Weaknesses
pronunciation	*pronunciation*
wording	*wording*
coherence / organization	*coherence / organization*
other	*other*

➡ Tips for EXTEND A GREETING QUESTIONS

1. You may want to use your pen and paper to jot down some key words or phrases.
2. Start with a simple greeting: *hi Carol, hello Joseph*. Speak clearly, and avoid filler sounds at the start.
3. Since you are role playing you are free to create a name and details that fit the context, such as type of new business. Keep your ideas simple. Talk about things you are familiar with.
4. Try to address all four parts of the question: offer a greeting, mention the new activity or event, share a positive reaction, and extend appropriate wishes.
5. Identify the relationship between you and the person you are speaking with. Choose appropriate language for the context. Consider level of formality, tone of voice, and choice of words.
6. Let both the words and the expression in your voice carry the positive reaction. *Congratulations! Wow! That's fantastic! Great, we really needed a business like that in our town!*
7. End with appropriate wishes: *Good luck on your new business. I hope your business does well. I wish you the best on your new business venture.*
8. Pause in grammatical places. Link the sounds within any single phrase. Include primary stress on each phrase, and alternate pitch between stressed and unstressed syllables. Use appropriate intonation curves for midsentence and sentence-final phrases.

Extend a Greeting Practice Questions

These practice questions will help you prepare to think quickly and respond concisely to *extend a greeting* questions. You should read each question and think about it for 30 seconds before answering the question. Feel free to write down a few notes during your 30-second preparation time, but do not try to write down everything you want to say. Work on one practice question at a time. If you preview all the questions at once, you will ruin the spontaneity. Make your practice as realistic as possible by not looking ahead at other questions and by keeping to the time limit. For each question below, record your responses. Then listen to each response to see if you have accurately responded to all parts of the question, and if you have appropriately addressed the intended audience. Correct and repeat responses that need improvement.

Practice Question 12.1

In this situation you will be asked to talk with a friend. Pretend that your friend has just recently been awarded an academic scholarship. Greet your friend and be sure to:

- say something about the scholarship,
- say something positive regarding the scholarship, and
- offer appropriate wishes to the friend.

Use the next 30 seconds to prepare your response. I will indicate when you should begin speaking. (preparation time = 30 seconds)

You may begin your response now. (60 seconds)

Practice Question 12.2

In this situation you will be asked to talk with a co-worker. Pretend that your co-worker has just recently published an article. Greet your co-worker and be sure to:

- say something about the article,
- say something positive regarding the article, and
- offer appropriate wishes to the co-worker.

Use the next 30 seconds to prepare your response. I will indicate when you should begin speaking. (preparation time = 60 seconds)

You may begin your response now. (60 seconds)

Practice Question 12.3

In this situation you will be asked to talk with a co-worker. Pretend that your co-worker has just recently received a research grant. Greet your co-worker and be sure to:

- say something about the research grant,
- say something positive regarding the grant, and
- offer appropriate wishes to the co-worker.

Use the next 30 seconds to prepare your response. I will indicate when you should begin speaking. (preparation time = 30 seconds)

You may begin your response now. (60 seconds)

Practice Question 12.4

In this situation you will be asked to talk with a co-worker. Pretend that your co-worker has just recently received a desirable overseas assignment. Greet your co-worker and be sure to:

- say something about the overseas assignment,
- say something positive regarding the overseas assignment, and
- offer appropriate wishes to the friend.

Use the next 30 seconds to prepare your response. I will indicate when you should begin speaking. (preparation time = 30 seconds)

Practice Question 12.5

In this situation you will be asked to talk with a friend. Pretend that your friend has just recently received a college degree. Greet your friend and be sure to:

- say something about the recent graduation,
- say something positive regarding the degree, and
- offer appropriate wishes to the friend.

Use the next 30 seconds to prepare your response. I will indicate when you should begin speaking. (preparation time = 30 seconds)

You may begin your response now. (60 seconds)

Practice Question 12.6

In this situation you will be asked to talk with a business associate. Pretend that your business associate has just recently received a large consulting contract. Greet your business associate and be sure to:

- say something about the large consulting contract,
- say something positive regarding the large consulting contract, and
- offer appropriate wishes to the business associate.

Use the next 30 seconds to prepare your response. I will indicate when you should begin speaking. (preparation time = 30 seconds)

You may begin your response now. (60 seconds)

Practice Question 12.7

In this situation you will be asked to talk with a co-worker. Pretend that your co-worker has just recently received an invitation to speak at an important professional conference. Greet your co-worker and be sure to:

- say something about the conference invitation,
- say something positive regarding the conference invitation, and
- offer appropriate wishes to the friend.

Use the next 30 seconds to prepare your response. I will indicate when you should begin speaking. (preparation time = 30 seconds)

You may begin your response now. (60 seconds)

Practice Question 12.8

In this situation you will be asked to talk with a colleague. Pretend that your colleague has just recently won a sales award. Greet your colleague and be sure to:

- say something about the sales award,
- say something positive regarding the sales award, and
- offer appropriate wishes to the colleague.

Use the next 30 seconds to prepare your response. I will indicate when you should begin speaking. (preparation time = 30 seconds)

You may begin your response now. (60 seconds)

Practice Question 12.9

In this situation you will be asked to talk with a friend. Pretend that your friend has just recently retired. Greet your friend and be sure to:

- say something about the retirement,
- say something positive regarding the retirement, and
- offer appropriate wishes to the friend.

Use the next 30 seconds to prepare your response. I will indicate when you should begin speaking. (preparation time = 30 seconds)

You may begin your response now. (60 seconds)

–13–

Respond to a Phone Message

In this chapter you will:

- Become familiar with the instructions for the *respond to a phone message* questions of the TSE®.
- See examples of *respond to a phone message* questions and corresponding responses.
- Learn what makes an effective response to *respond to a phone message* questions.
- Practice responding to a variety of *respond to a phone message* questions.

The general directions for the *respond to a phone message* question are the same as for the *extend a greeting* question presented in Chapter 12. A successful response will take into consideration what the situation is and to whom you are speaking. The context will most likely be a business, commercial, or industrial setting, although it could be an academic or social setting as well. The relationship of the person you pretend to talk with will be defined in the question, such as business colleague, unknown company representative, work supervisor, new acquaintance, peer, or friend.

For the *respond to a phone message* questions, you hear a telephone message and you pretend to call back with a response. The phone message is heard, it is not written in the test booklet. Since your ability to listen and remember what you hear will affect how well you respond, you may want to take notes. You are free to take notes during any portion of the test, but you may find it most helpful for the questions with listening passages. If you do take notes it is best to write key words or short phrases and then to briefly order these for your response. Don't try to write out everything you want to say; you won't have time. Use the notes to trigger your memory so that you can focus on speaking fluently. If taking notes distracts you, then do not take notes.

The *respond to a phone message* question may be something like this:

In this situation you will hear and respond to a telephone message containing a complaint. Pretend that you are the manager of an apartment rental company. After the message is played you will have 30 seconds to think about a response. Your response should:

   a. **demonstrate that you understand the caller's problem, and**
   b. **suggest a solution to the problem that would satisfy the caller.**

Please listen to the voice message.

(On the TSE®, the voice message will be played aloud. It will not be written as it is here.)

Hello. My name is Ellen Harrison. Last week I moved into apartment B in the Green Street Apartments. I was told that the loose tiles on the kitchen floor and the leaky faucet in the bathroom would be fixed within three days. The repairperson came yesterday to fix the tiles, and it looks really nice. But I haven't seen the plumber yet, and the dripping from the faucet is driving me crazy at night when I am trying to sleep. Please call me back today, and let me know how you're going to take care of this. I tried calling all weekend but kept getting your answering machine. The leak is getting worse

everyday, and I don't want to have to worry about this problem anymore.

....

You may now take 30 seconds to think about your response
to the caller. I will tell you when you can start recording
your response. (preparation time = 30 seconds)

Please begin your response now. (60 seconds)

The question is written in the test booklet, and a short message is played
aloud without any supporting text. Here is an example of a phone message:

***This call is for Ellen Harrison / um / this is the manager of
the Green Street apartments / I'm very sorry that your
lof / your faucet is still dripping / um / our person who's
supposed to be here over the weekend was out of town /
(cough) um / we'll try to get someone over there as soon as
we can / uh to fix this leaky faucet / um in the meantime I
hope you can just bear it / we'll hope someone / could get
over there / uh / this afternoon / I again I wanna apologize
for the inconvenience that this is causing you Ellen***
(20 seconds remaining)

It is common to greet the person you are leaving a message for at the beginning of the message. This response does that clearly by stating, *This call is
for Ellen Harrison.* When listening to the message, be sure to note the name
of the person calling so you can use his or her name in your response. Listen to the pronunciation of the name so you can pronounce it correctly. In
this situation you want to avoid calling *Ellen Helen* or *Allan,* or something
else by mistake. If you realize you don't remember the name, give a friendly
greeting anyway and identify yourself. In this response the speaker identifies her position as manager of the apartments. Alternatively you could give

your name, or a made up name for the response, along with your position, such as *I'm Jane McDonald, the manager of the Green Street Apartments.*

The speaker's tone is familiar and understanding throughout the response. This familiarity is conveyed by using the person's name at the beginning and end. She also uses a number of contractions to add to the informality, such as: *I'm, who's,* and *we'll.* Using the reduced form *wanna* instead of *want to* also makes the tone sound familiar. *I'm very sorry that your faucet is still dripping* sounds more familiar than just *Sorry your faucet is dripping.* The phrasing and tone help to create a friendly, collaborative feeling rather than a confrontational one.

The speaker shows sympathy for the caller's complaint by saying, *I'm very sorry that your faucet is still dripping.* Another way to show sympathy is to identify with the caller's dilemma by saying something like, *I know how irritating a dripping faucet can be,* or *I once had a dripping faucet and I didn't get any rest until it was fixed.* The speaker goes on to explain why the problem hasn't been fixed yet. This shows that the manager does care and hasn't forgotten about this problem.

All of these are preliminaries before presenting a solution to the problem. If the greeting, self identification, expression of sympathy, and explanation of what's been done up until now are skipped over, the message will seem abrupt to the listener. Although the speaker proposes a solution, she adds some tentative expressions like *we'll try, as soon as we can, I hope,* and *we'll hope.* Speaking in cautious terms like this can discourage future complaints if the help doesn't come as soon as was hoped for. This type of response can also backfire if the listener interprets the tentative language as a lack of commitment to solve the problem now. Yet this speaker's response seems reasonable, and if the help arrives before too long, then everyone should be happy. The speaker ends the message politely by reinforcing her apology.

An appropriate pattern to follow for responding to a complaint is:

- extend a greeting;
- identify yourself and your position;
- show sympathy for the person's situation;
- explain what has been done up until now;

- propose a solution with details about who will be doing what when; and
- close by repeating important information, like a time and date when help will arrive, or by apologizing and promising to help.

Here is another example response:

> *Miss Harrison / I want to thank you for your call and I wish to uh / just apologize that nobody got out there over the weekend um / for the leaky faucet / over there at apartment 3B on Green Street / I understand uh / the tiles were / were fixed and I'm glad that happened um / as far as the / the leaky faucet is concerned I'm goin to get a verbal guarantee from him that he's going to be out there in the next day or two / uh / again I'm sorry our our weekend guy was out of town / so we're actually gonna call / call a plumber to get him out there today* (26 seconds remaining)

In this response the speaker uses the last name instead of the first name, which makes the message sound a little more formal. The expression *I want to thank you*, especially in reference to a complaint sounds overly formal. Before going into the problem, the speaker mentions the point they both are happy about, *the tiles were fixed*. At first the speaker is hoping to get a plumber within *the next day or two*, but by the end promises *to get him out there today*. In the previous two example responses there was ample time remaining at the end. This suggests that these speakers might think for a few seconds before starting their response, which might result in fewer hesitations or restatements.

⚙ Exercise 13.1: Identifying the Pattern of a Response

Write the corresponding phrase from the previous example response for each of the sections below.

1. Extend a greeting:

   _____

   _____

2. Identify yourself and your position:

   _____

   _____

3. Show sympathy for the person's situation:

   _____

   _____

4. Explain what has been done up until now:

   _____

   _____

5. Propose a solution with details about who will be doing what when:

   _____

   _____

6. Close by repeating important information, like a time and date when help will arrive, or by apologizing and promising to help:

   _____

   _____

Here is another example response. Write the corresponding phrase for each of the sections below.

> *Hello, is this Ellen / my name is Colleen / I'm from the rental company / I got our message / but I'm sorry that uh / our an / our message system didn't work during the weekends / uh / mm / I learned ther / I understand that the leaking problem is annoying you / a lot / and uh / make t / and brings trouble to your life / I'm awfully sorry about that / I have send a person / to resolve this problem you should hear from / you you should see him / uh this afternoon / if not please call me again / I assure you / I / you will have a good sleep tonight / th the it will / the leaking problem will (won't) alloy (annoy) you any more / so / uh / again / please / uh / again pl . . .*

1. Extend a greeting:

_____

_____

2. Identify yourself and your position:

_____

_____

3. Show sympathy for the person's situation:

_____

_____

4. Explain what has been done up until now:

_____

_____

5. Propose a solution with details about who will be doing what when:

_____

_____

6. Close by repeating important information, like a time and date when help will arrive, or by apologizing and promising to help:

_____

_____

Here is another example response:

> *Okay / hello Ellen / I am calling for your rent-al office / I hear about your complaint / we were / trying to solve that in / last week but / we we / we were not be able to reach a efficient plumber for / to repair your problem so / at this point we think / we found one that will be / there probably next week / what we can do during this time is / maybe make some kind of provisional repair / to try to / I don't know ha / to / low the noise of this / uh that this particular problem has interrupt apartment but / we can not do any / any thing more so / try / the only solution that we have is just wait until next week that we can solve the problem / we will be able to solve that /*

This speaker suggests a complex solution of a temporary repair now and a permanent fix in a week from now. While this is a valid response, it seems like the speaker is struggling to explain this approach, especially in this phrase: *to try to, I don't know ha, to, low the noise of this.* It's hard to imagine what a temporary fix might be—turn off the water supply, close the bathroom door, put a sponge in the sink to catch the drips? Since there is not enough detail provided from the speaker, the listener is left guessing what is really meant. Furthermore, the raters may not take into account that the language for a complex solution could be more difficult to generate than the language for a simple solution. Also by delaying the permanent repair for a week, the listener may be left with the impression that the speaker can't accomplish this task easily. Even though the speaker gets his point across, he may be more successful by suggesting a simple solution in a clear, concise manner.

Exercise 13.2: Correcting Grammar

The sentences below were taken from the previous example response. Rewrite each sentence in correct grammatical form. Reword for brevity and clarity as needed. Say each corrected sentence aloud as fluently as you can by focusing on alternations of stressed and unstressed syllables, primary stress, and intonation.

1. I hear about your complaint.

_____

_____

2. We were trying to solve that in last week.

_____

_____

3. We were not be able to reach a efficient plumber for to repair your problem.

_____

_____

4. What we can do during this time is maybe make some kind of provisional repair to try to, I don't know, to low the noise of this that this particular problem has interrupt apartment.

_____

_____

5. So try the only solution that we have is just wait until next week that we can solve the problem.

_____

_____

Here is another example response:

> *Ellen / I'm very sorry because I was out of town / uh / in during the last several days so I can't answer / your / uh / requests very prom / very timely / and now I I should give you a very / uh / try to give you a satisfactory answer / to your problem / first of I should / express our apology for / uh / our / just some / carelessness / or / delay for the / uh / for the main / uh / for the fix / for the fix of the the leaking faucet / and uh / I just uh / assure you that we / uh / we were going to just send some people to make it / uh / right now / and uh / and uh / so / the I I I'm quite sure the problem will be solved very soon*

This speaker uses the person's name and extends an apology. When the speaker forgets the word *promptly*, he changes to the word *timely*, which works just as well. The phrase *now I should try to give you a satisfactory answer* sounds a bit stiff and formal. Likewise, rather than say, *first I should express our apology*, the speaker could directly say, *I apologize that the leaky faucet hasn't been repaired sooner*. The phrase *we were going to just send some people* sounds like this was the speaker's initial idea but maybe the plan has changed. This could be rephrased as *we are sending over a repair person immediately* or *we are going to send a repair person as soon as I finish this call.* The use of *we* can help take the blame off the individual speaking and lets the speaker appear to be working with the caller. In this response the speaker switches back and forth between *I* and *we*. Although this speaker accomplishes the task of responding to the message, communication is weakened by repetitions, phrasing, and tone.

---

⑤ Exercise 13.3: Expressing an Apology

Here are some useful expressions for expressing an apology:

- *I'm sorry.*
- *I'm very sorry.*
- *I'm really sorry.*
- *I'm terribly sorry.*
- *Please forgive me.*
- *I'll have someone take care of that.*
- *I'll have someone look into that.*
- *I'll have that taken care of right away.*
- *I apologize for . . . .*

You may also hear the expressions excuse me *or* pardon me; *these are used when interrupting or disturbing someone rather than as apologies.*

For each of the situations below, write an apology. In addition to the words expressing regret, you may also want to include a reason for the situation. The first one has been done for you. Say each apology aloud with a sincere tone.

1. You arrive late for a business meeting.

   I'm really sorry for coming late. There was an accident on
   the toll road, and it backed up traffic for half an hour.

2. You can't get the report to your boss by the deadline.

_____

_____

3. You accidentally hit another car parked on the street.

_____

_____

4. You can't help a colleague with a computer problem this weekend as you originally planned.

_____

_____

5. You promised to call a client with the results of a lab test, but you forgot.

_____

_____

6. Your company didn't make a profit this year so there won't be any employee bonuses at the end of the year.

_____

_____

●→ Tips for RESPOND TO A TELEPHONE MESSAGE QUESTIONS

1. You may want to use your pen and paper to jot down some key words or phrases, such as names, places, times, etc.

2. Include all six parts of an effective phone message response, including: greeting, self identification, expression of sympathy, explanation of past actions, proposed solution, and a closing.

3. In the greeting use the person's name to create an informal, friendly mood.

4. In the self identification, you can state your name or a pretend name and your position for the role-play.

5. Let both the words and the expression in your voice convey sympathy, apology, regret regarding the problem, as well as confidence and certainty in your solution.

6. Reinforce that you do care by explaining the actions you've already taken on behalf of the caller.

7. Keep your solution simple, and explain it clearly.

8. Close by repeating your apology or by summarizing the key points to your solution.

9. Pause in grammatical places. Link the sounds within any single phrase. Include primary stress on each phrase, and alternate pitch between stressed and unstressed syllables. Use appropriate intonation for phrases that end in the middle of sentences and for phrases at the end of sentences.

Respond to a Phone Message Practice Questions

These practice questions will help you prepare to think quickly and respond concisely to *respond to a phone message* type questions. On the TSE® you would normally hear the questions without being able to read them. In this practice section you will be able to see the messages in written form. For practice you should read each question and think about it for 30 seconds before answering. Feel free to write down a few notes during your 30-second preparation time, but do not try to write down everything you want to say. Work on one practice question at a time. If you preview all the questions at once, you will ruin the spontaneity. Make your practice as realistic as possible by not looking ahead at other questions and by keeping to the time limit. For each practice question, record your response. Then listen to each response to see if you have accurately responded to all parts of the question, and if you have appropriately addressed the intended audience. Correct and repeat responses that need improvement.

Practice Question 13.1

In this situation you will hear and respond to a telephone message containing a complaint. Pretend that you are the manager of a car rental agency. After the message is played, you will have 30 seconds to think about a response. Your response should:

    a. demonstrate that you understand the caller's problem, and

    b. suggest a solution to the problem that would satisfy the caller.

Please listen to the voice message.

• •

Voice Message

(On the TSE® this message will be played aloud; it will not be written as it is here.)

Robert: Hello. My name is Robert Gardner. Just this morning I came to your office to rent a car for my business trip downstate. After driving for only a half hour the car started overheating and finally stalled. I was finally able to contact a garage who towed the car in. Now they are telling me it will take two days to fix. Before I picked up this car I was told that it was given a thorough check over. I've called three times already today. I need another rental car, and I need it now. You can call me back on my cell phone.

Narrator: You may now take 30 seconds to think about your response to the caller. I will tell you when you can start recording your response. (preparation time = 30 seconds)

Please begin your response now. (60 seconds)

• •

Practice Question 13.2

In this situation you will hear and respond to a telephone message containing a complaint. Pretend that you are the manager of the local newspaper company. After the message is played, you will have 30 seconds to think about a response. Your response should:

    a. demonstrate that you understand the caller's problem, and
    b. suggest a solution to the problem that would satisfy the caller.

Please listen to the voice message.

Voice Message
(On the TSE® this message will be played aloud; it will not be written as it is here.)

Chris: Hello. My name is Chris Coleman. Apparently there is a new person delivering the morning newspaper. Every day this week I've had to hunt for the paper. One time it was behind the bushes, and another time it was on top of the bushes. But this morning my newspaper was thrown into my flower garden and destroyed a bunch of my flowers. I've had enough of this. If the newspaper doesn't wind up on my front doormat, I'm canceling my subscription. Please call me back today and let me know how you're going to take care of this.

Narrator: You may now take 30 seconds to think about your response to the caller. I will tell you when you can start recording your response. (preparation time = 30 seconds)

Please begin your response now. (60 seconds)

Practice Question 13.3

In this situation you will hear and respond to a telephone message containing a complaint. Pretend that you are the manager of the trash company. After the message is played, you will have 30 seconds to think about a response. Your response should:

    a. demonstrate that you understand the caller's problem, and

    b. suggest a solution to the problem that would satisfy the caller.

Please listen to the voice message. (60 seconds)

Voice Message
(On the TSE® this message will be played aloud; it will not be written as it is here.)

Susan: Hello. My name is Susan Farnsworth. Your company has been picking up trash from my house for over five years. But lately there have been a lot of problems. Apparently not all the trash is getting into the truck, and litter is left on my front lawn. In addition there are large dents in my trash can, and the lid doesn't even fit on any more. This has been very frustrating, to say the least. We are never late paying our trash bill; I think we deserve better service than this. Please call me back today and let me know how you're going to take care of this. I called and left a message yesterday, but no one has called me back.

Narrator: You may now take 30 seconds to think about your response to the caller. I will tell you when you can start recording your response. (preparation time = 30 seconds)

Please begin your response now. (60 seconds)

Practice Question 13.4

In this situation you will hear and respond to a telephone message containing a request. Pretend that you are a hotel manager. After the message is played, you will have 30 seconds to think about a response. Your response should:

a. demonstrate that you understand the caller's problem, and
b. suggest a solution to the problem that would satisfy the caller.

Please listen to the voice message.

Voice Message
(On the TSE® this message will be played aloud; it will not be written as it is here.)

Jessica: Hello. My name is Jessica Lundell. I have reservations for the middle of the month. We were intending on celebrating our anniversary with a small vacation. I sent in my nonrefundable deposit last week. Unfortunately, my travel plans have changed. I can't get away from work until the end of the summer. Is there any way I could get my deposit back? I know it's your policy not to give refunds for cancellations, but I'm hoping that because I'm calling so early that you can make some accommodations. I'm really disappointed to cancel this trip, but I really can't afford to lose this money. Could you call me back later today and let me know what you think? Thanks.

Narrator: You may now take 30 seconds to think about your response to the caller. I will tell you when you can start recording your response. (preparation time = 30 seconds)

Please begin your response now. (60 seconds)

Practice Question 13.5

In this situation you will hear and respond to a telephone message containing a complaint. Pretend that you are a bank loan officer. After the message is played, you will have 30 seconds to think about a response. Your response should:

a. demonstrate that you understand the caller's problem, and

b. suggest a solution to the problem that would satisfy the caller.

Please listen to the voice message. (60 seconds)

● ●

Voice Message

(On the TSE® this message will be played aloud; it will not be written as it is here.)

David: Hello. My name is David Griswold. Two weeks ago you helped me fill out the paperwork for a home mortgage. You said I needed to supply copies of my bank statements and verification of employment. I dropped all that off last week. I really need to know if the loan is approved or not. We are trying to schedule a closing date on a house. But the owner is getting anxious because we haven't been approved for a loan yet. Could you please check the status of our loan request and give me a call back at work? Thanks.

Narrator: You may now take 30 seconds to think about your response to the caller. I will tell you when you can start recording your response. (preparation time = 30 seconds)

Please begin your response now. (60 seconds)

● ●

Practice Question 13.6

In this situation you will hear and respond to a telephone message containing a complaint. Pretend that you are a clerk at a pharmacy. After the message is played, you will have 30 seconds to think about a response. Your response should:

    a. demonstrate that you understand the caller's problem, and
    b. suggest a solution to the problem that would satisfy the caller.

Please listen to the voice message.

Voice Message
(On the TSE® this message will be played aloud; it will not be written as it is here.)

Kara: Hello. This is Kara Payne. I need the medicine that the doctor prescribed for me. I was sick all night, and I seem to be getting worse every minute. I dropped off the two prescriptions the doctor gave me after I saw her this morning. You said you'd call me when they were ready to be picked up. I left messages at noon and at two, but I never heard back from you. Now it's almost four o'clock, and I really need those prescriptions. I don't know what the problem is, but I can't wait much longer. Bye.

Narrator: You may now take 30 seconds to think about your response to the caller. I will tell you when you can start recording your response. (preparation time = 30 seconds)

Please begin your response now. (60 seconds)

Practice Question 13.7

In this situation you will hear and respond to a telephone message containing a complaint. Pretend that you are a nurse in a doctor's office. After the message is played, you will have 30 seconds to think about a response. Your response should:

a. demonstrate that you understand the caller's problem, and

b. suggest a solution to the problem that would satisfy the caller.

Please listen to the voice message.

••

Voice Message

(On the TSE® this message will be played aloud; it will not be written as it is here.)

Dennis: Hello. This is Dennis Stanford, I was in two days ago. Dr. Clark looked at a really bad rash I have and prescribed some ointment. I've been applying the ointment every six hours like he said, but it just gets worse and worse. Not only that, I feel sick to my stomach. He said the medication should start working within 24 hours. I'm beginning to worry because it's just gotten worse. I left a message earlier this morning, but I really need to set up another appointment with Dr. Clark for this afternoon. Please call me back on my cell phone. Bye.

Narrator: You may now take 30 seconds to think about your response to the caller. I will tell you when you can start recording your response. (preparation time = 30 seconds)

Please begin your response now. (60 seconds)

••

Practice Question 13.8

In this situation you will hear and respond to a telephone message containing a complaint. Pretend that you are a representative from an insurance company. After the message is played, you will have 30 seconds to think about a response. Your response should:

a. demonstrate that you understand the caller's problem, and

b. suggest a solution to the problem that would satisfy the caller.

Please listen to the voice message.

Voice Message

(On the TSE® this message will be played aloud; it will not be written as it is here.)

Valerie: Hello. I'm Valerie Wilkinson, my insurance number is 87-346222. I just got a letter in the mail from your company that said my insurance would not be covering the emergency room visit or the x-rays from last month. I understood that the policy would cover 50 percent of the emergency room visit and all of the x-rays. I had to pay the hospital for the full cost of everything at the time of the incident. I don't have a lot of extra money, and I really need to get reimbursed right away. Could you take a look at my file and call me back? I'll be out between 1:30 and 3:00, but you can call after that. Thanks.

Narrator: You may now take 30 seconds to think about your response to the caller. I will tell you when you can start recording your response. (preparation time = 30 seconds)

Please begin your response now. (60 seconds)

Practice Question 13.9

In this situation you will hear and respond to a telephone message containing a complaint. Pretend that you are a financial aid officer at a university. After the message is played, you will have 30 seconds to think about a response. Your response should:

a. demonstrate that you understand the caller's problem, and

b. suggest a solution to the problem that would satisfy the caller.

Please listen to the voice message.

Voice Message

(On the TSE® this message will be played aloud; it will not be written as it is here.)

Graham: Hello. My name is Graham Jennings. My son is Jeffrey Jennings; he's a junior. A letter from the University arrived two days ago saying he was denied financial aid for this semester. He has been getting financial aid all along, so I don't know what the deal is. We resubmitted his financial aid application the same way as before. Everything was in on time. He's always gotten good grades, so I really don't know what the problem could be. We really can't afford not to get financial aid. I left a message yesterday, but haven't heard back from anyone yet. Could you give me a call so we can straighten things out? Thanks.

Narrator: You may now take 30 seconds to think about your response to the caller. I will tell you when you can start recording your response. (preparation time = 30 seconds)

Please begin your response now. (60 seconds)

Practice Question 13.10

In this situation you will hear and respond to a telephone message containing a complaint. Pretend that you are the director of operations and maintenance. After the message is played, you will have 30 seconds to think about a response. Your response should:

a. demonstrate that you understand the caller's problem, and

b. suggest a solution to the problem that would satisfy the caller.

Please listen to the voice message.

Voice Message
(On the TSE® this message will be played aloud; it will not be written as it is here.)

Evelyne: Hello. This is Evelyne Sellers. I work in the Administration Building, east wing, third floor. Yesterday it was extremely warm over here. We turned on the air conditioning. Air was blowing, but it wasn't cool air. Today the air conditioning has been blowing cold air all morning and no matter what we do to the thermostat, the cold air just keeps coming. It's 67 degrees in here right now. Everyone's wearing a sweater or jacket, and we're still freezing. I talked with the people on the floors above and below me, but everything seems to be fine there. Please give me a call as soon as you can and let me know what can be done. Thanks.

Narrator: You may now take 30 seconds to think about your response to the caller. I will tell you when you can start recording your response. (preparation time = 30 seconds)

Please begin your response now. (60 seconds)

–14–

Give a Progress Report

> In this chapter you will:
>
> - Become familiar with the instructions for the *give a progress report* questions of the TSE®.
> - See examples of *give a progress report* questions and corresponding responses.
> - Learn what makes an effective response to *give a progress report* questions.
> - Practice responding to a variety of *give a progress report* questions.

The general directions for the *give a progress report* question are the same as for the *extend a greeting* question presented in Chapter 12. A successful response will take into consideration what the situation is and to whom you are speaking. The context will most likely be a business, commercial, or industrial setting, though it could be an academic or social setting as well. The relationship of the person you pretend to talk with will be defined in the question, such as a work supervisor or client.

For the *give a progress report* questions you are shown a visual, like a flow chart of a business process, and are allowed to study it for 15 seconds. You will also hear a dialogue that provides specific details related to the visual. The dialogue is heard, not written in the test booklet. You have 45 seconds to prepare an answer and 60 seconds to deliver your progress report based on the information in the visual and the dialogue.

Since your ability to listen and remember what you hear will affect how well you respond, you may want to take notes. You are free to take notes during any portion of the test, but you may find it most helpful for the questions with listening passages. If you do take notes, it is best to write key words or short phrases and then to briefly order these for your response. Don't try to write out everything you want to say; you won't have time. Use the notes to trigger your memory so that you can focus on speaking fluently. If taking notes distracts you, then do not take notes.

The *give a progress report* question may be something like this:

> **Along with a flow chart you will hear a conversation between two people. Based on that information, you will be asked to make an oral progress report as if you were leaving a voice-mail message on the telephone. Pretend that you work in the human resources division of an organization that is going through the hiring process. You will have the next 15 seconds to review the flowchart that outlines the hiring process.** (preparation time = 15 seconds)

Hiring Process

Management team makes decision to hire

↓

Committee advertises position

↓

Committee reviews resumes

↓

Committee selects candidates to interview

↓

Committee conducts interviews

↓

Committee drafts recommendations

↓

Management gives approval

In a moment you will hear two people talking about the company hiring process. When the conversation is completed, you will have 45 seconds to prepare a voice-mail progress report for your supervisor, Mr. Richland. Please listen to the conversation.

•••

(On the TSE® the dialogue will be played aloud; it will not be written as it is here.)

Maria: Hi, Andrew! Have you made any progress on filling that job opening?

Andrew: You won't believe it; it's been quite a job. That committee takes up more of my time than anything else right now.

Maria: Did many people apply?

Andrew: Exactly! That's the problem. We received over 100 resumes, and each committee member had to review each one. It took forever, but we finally narrowed it down to three candidates.

Maria: When will the interviews be?

Andrew: Actually, we held two of the interviews yesterday, and the third one is on Friday. I've been in charge of arranging to give each candidate a company tour, so I've gotten to know each one fairly well so far.

Maria: When will the final decision be made?

Andrew: The committee will meet early next week to prepare a recommendation for the management team. If everything goes smoothly, we should have a new worker on the job before the busy season starts.

Maria: That would be great. I'll bet you'll be happy when this process is over.

Andrew: I've learned a lot during the process, but I'll definitely be glad when it's over.

•••

Use the next 45 seconds to prepare your report for Mr. Richland. In your report be sure to:

- describe what the situation is,
- explain what has been accomplished, and
- report what is left to be done.

Do not begin your progress report voice-mail until you are instructed to do so. (preparation time = 45 seconds)

You may begin your response now. (60 seconds)

As you listen to the dialogue, try to place the specific information into the outline of the general information shown on the visual. Be sure to note names, dates, and places accurately. If you don't remember some specific details, it will be hard to give an effective report. On the other hand, it is not necessary to remember every detail. The test is not a memory test. If there are a few details that escaped you, don't worry. Focus on clearly talking about the details you do remember. The question itself suggests an appropriate outline for your response: describe the situation, explain what has been done, and what still needs to be done.

Here is an example response:

Mr. Richland / I'm just calling to get a hold of you and to give you an update / (cough) on the current hiring situation going on in human resources / we / ehm received over one hundred applications / to the committee and we've reviewed them all / and uh the committee has narrowed them down to three candidates / uh we are currently conducting interviews / two of them are already done / and uh the third one is slotted for Friday / Andrew has been giving those three candidates tours um / the last one / uh / during his inter or before his interview is going to get the tour this Friday / turns out we should have uh / the committee meeting

> *next week for recommendations we hope to have one*
> *produced by the end of the week / and then um / depending*
> *on how long the management approval process takes we*
> *expect to get a / a new hire before the busy season / uh / so*
> *Mr. Ro Richland just wanted to give you that update /*
> *um feel free to contact me if you've got any questions*

This response begins with the person's last name preceded by the formal title *Mr.* to show respect, even though in many offices today, workers and supervisors use first names to address one another. The caller gets down to business right away as indicated by the absence of a greeting like *Hello* or *Hi, Mr. Richland*. If the last name is spoken alone with a sharp or flat tone, it could give the impression of anger or dominance. Proper alternations of stressed and unstressed syllables as this speaker used help to keep the tone friendly, yet professional. The addition of *hello* or *hi* is not necessary but could add a friendlier, more polite tone.

In the first sentence the speaker identifies his reason for calling: *to give you an update on the current hiring situation going on in human resources.* The speaker first reviews what has been done and then goes on to talk about what remains to be done. This organizational structure follows the suggested outline from the question prompt. Key points are discussed, such as number of applicants, number of candidates, scheduling of interviews, company tours, and committee recommendations. The presentation of these points is organized according to the steps in the process. Details are accurately and concisely expressed, such as: *we received over one hundred applications, narrowed them down to three candidates, currently conducting interviews,* and *a new hire before the busy season.* The speaker reminds the listener that the approval process depends on management's review, but also sounds hopeful that they will successfully hire someone before the busy season begins. The conclusion extends an offer to respond to any remaining questions, which is common in business correspondence.

The following is a list of typical elements that can be found in an oral progress report. Not all elements need be in every report.

- Extend a greeting.
- Identify yourself and your position.

- Identify the purpose of your call.
- Give the main conclusion of your report if known.
- Summarize the important steps that have been accomplished.
- Summarize the important steps that have yet to be accomplished.
- Ask the caller for advice or help.
- Close with emphasizing the main idea or by offering to provide more details.

Here is another example response:

> *Mr. Richland / this is Renee Browning / uh / in the human resource division / I just wanted to fill you in on what's going on here / right now um / we received over a hundred applicants to the position / and we've narrowed it down to three / two of them were interviewed yesterday / and the third will be interviewed later this week / um / the committee should have a recommendation early next week and / we hope to have the position filled before the busy season begins /* (23 seconds remaining)

This speaker also begins with the supervisor's title and last name, *Mr. Richland.* She goes on to identify herself and her position. The body of the response focuses on key points without going into small details. She mentions the applications but doesn't say that each committee member read each application. She mentions the interviews but doesn't mention the company tours given by Andrew. She mentions when the committee's recommendation should be ready but doesn't mention the need for management's approval. By focusing on the major points and skipping over the minor details, this speaker finishes in about half the time allotted. The response was spoken with excellent alternations, primary stress, and intonation and would be considered a strong response. If the delivery were not as strong, this speaker might consider talking about more details and using more of the response time to better illustrate her communication ability.

⏏ Exercise 14.1: Identifying the Elements of a Response

Write the corresponding phrase from the previous example response for each of the sections that follow. Not all sections are represented in each example.

1. Extend a greeting:

   _____

   _____

2. Identify yourself and your position:

   _____

   _____

3. Identify the purpose of your call:

   _____

   _____

4. Give the main conclusion of your report if known:

   _____

   _____

5. Summarize the important steps that have been accomplished:

   _____

   _____

6. Summarize the important steps that have yet to be accomplished:

   _____

   _____

7. Ask the caller for advice or help:

_____

_____

8. Close with emphasizing the main idea or by offering to provide more details:

_____

_____

Here is another example response. Write the corresponding phrase for each of the sections.

Hi Mr. / Mr. Richland this is Sharon from the company hiring committee / recently we are working on / the process / hire a new staff / for our company / uh we / we received one hundred resumes / this is a lot of / this is a big number of applications / and each committee uh read through one resumes and finally we / got three committees (candidates) / in last ə Friday we interviewed two / and we h / we still have one / I need to interviews / so / uh / if / and Andrew / uh show / uh guide the a / applycant (applicant) / a a tour / in the in the company / so if everything goes smoothly we will get a decision / uh in the early next week / and we will / uh find a new / uh / new work partner in our lab / in our company

---

1. Extend a greeting:

_____

_____

2. Identify yourself and your position:

_____

_____

3. Identify the purpose of your call:

_____

_____

4. Give the main conclusion of your report if known:

_____

_____

5. Summarize the important steps that have been accomplished:

_____

_____

6. Summarize the important steps that have yet to be accomplished:

_____

_____

7. Ask the caller for advice or help:

_____

_____

8. Close with emphasizing the main idea or by offering to provide more details:

_____

_____

Here is another example response:

> **This time we accepted more than / uh / we we accepted
> hundreds of applications / right now the situation the
> committee has selected three candidates for the / opening
> job / and uh / uh / yesterday the committee held two
> interviews with interview / interviewers / and they are
> going to have / one more interview on Friday / and uh /
> the committee is planning to give / all the candidates a
> touring / over the company / and uh so / uh / if everything
> is ok / uh in the early days / of next week the committee
> will finish the / uh / the recommendation draft / and uh /
> will send it to the manager approver / so we hope that /
> the / the job will be fused (finished) before the b- / b- uh /
> busy season / (pause) / that's my report**

This response jumps right into the details of the process, which weakens the coherence of the response. This requires listeners to listen for awhile before they can determine which situation is being described. Imagine picking up the phone in the middle of a conversation or hearing a conversation of two people walking past you. You may be able to understand some of what is being said, but it is difficult to interpret and understand without knowing the context. This response could be made stronger by starting with a greeting and identification of self, followed by a brief statement identifying the situation being discussed.

The general meaning is conveyed in this response, but a number of phrases could be reworded for clarity. For example, *opening job* could be phrased as *job opening; two interviews with interviewers* could be phrased as *met with two interviewees* (or *job candidates); a touring over the company* could be rephrased to *give a company tour; in the early days of next week* could be rephrased to *early next week* or *in the first half of next week;* and *send to the manager approver* could be rephrased to *send to management for approval.*

Here is another example response:

> *Mr. Richland / the interview for the current opening / uh*
> *has / has not finish-ed yet / but three candidates / pick-ed*
> *out / two have been interviewed yesterday / and uh one*
> *will be interviewed uh / this Friday / during the previous*
> *couple of weeks / there / were / around one hundred persons*
> *who applied for this opening / the committeer / the*
> *committee member has / uh / one by one / and they*
> *selected three candidates / as I mentioned they / have /*
> *they have or will have been / interviewed / and the*
> *decision / Andrew will give the / to / will give the tour for*
> *ther / for the interviewees*

This speaker begins appropriately and touches upon the main points of a job opening—three candidates interviewed, around 100 applicants, and a company tour for the interviewees. The speaker generally uses rise-to-mid-range intonation for mid-sentence phrases and low-range intonation for ends of sentences. However, the information is hard to follow because a number of ideas are left incomplete. For example, *the committee member has one by one* is not enough to explain that the committee members all looked at each of the resumes. The phrase *and the decision* is left hanging without any details of when or how a decision will be reached. It is unclear if the speaker forgot these details or just didn't know how to express them. Mentioning the tour after bringing up the decision is confusing because the tours come before the decision chronologically.

⑤ Exercise 14.2: Correcting Grammar

The sentences below were taken from the previous example response. Rewrite each sentence in correct grammatical form. Reword for brevity and clarity as needed. Say each corrected sentence aloud as fluently as you can by focusing on alternations of stressed and unstressed syllables, primary stress, and intonation. The first one has been done for you.

1. The interview for the current opening has not finished yet.

   <u>All the interviews for the current opening have not been finished yet.</u>

2. But three candidates picked out, two have been interviewed yesterday and one will be interviewed this Friday.

   _____

   _____

3. The committee member has, one by one, and they selected three candidates.

   _____

   _____

4. As I mentioned they have or will have been interviewed and the decision.

   _____

   _____

💬 Exercise 14.3: Analyzing Verb Tense Use

In this exercise you are given a paragraph adapted from an example response. Notice the mix of past, present, and future tenses. Different verb tenses are used for different reasons. For each verb listed, write a brief note to explain why the tense was used.

Hi, Mr. Richland, I'd like to give you a brief progress report on the hiring process for the open position. There were more than one hundred people who applied for this job. We spent a lot of time reading their resumes. We narrowed this down to a short list of three names. Two candidates were interviewed yesterday, and the third will be interviewed on Friday. Andrew is giving a company tour to each of the candidates. Early next week the search committee will meet to finalize a recommendation for management's review and approval. If all goes well, we should have a new employee before busy season.

1. I'd like to give . . .

   <u>This indicates a wish or desire for the future.</u>

   _____

2. there were more . . .

   _____

   _____

3. who applied . . .

_____

_____

4. we spent . . .

_____

_____

5. narrowed this down to . . .

_____

_____

6. will be interviewed . . .

_____

_____

7. Andrew is giving . . .

_____

_____

8. will meet . . .

_____

_____

9. If all goes well . . .

_____

_____

10. we should have . . .

_____

_____

🔊 Exercise 14.4: Pronouncing Words with *-ed* Endings

Many verbs use -ed to form past tense. Generally when past tense -ed follows a /t/ or a /d/ sound, then -ed is pronounced as a syllable and a consonant, /əd/. Otherwise /ed/ is generally pronounced as a single consonant, either /t/ or /d/. One error that some speakers make is to leave off -ed endings when needed. This might be a grammar error or it might be a pronunciation error. Another common mistake is to mispronounce the single consonant /ed/ sound as a vowel and consonant. Mistakes with /ed/ endings can make a speaker sound immature, or they can lead to misunderstandings.

Say each of the following phrases aloud while focusing on correctly pronouncing the -ed endings.

1. omitted details
2. collected data
3. viewed on-line
4. learned it last week
5. required references
6. compared cost and reliability
7. selected problems
8. provided resources
9. operated the equipment
10. practiced frequently

Say each of the phrases again in a sentence that you create.

⟳ Exercise 14.5: Describing a Past Event

Record yourself describing a past event you took part in. You could talk about a trip you took last summer or what you did last weekend. Listen to your recording, and identify all the past tense verbs with -ed. Check to see that you pronounced each correctly. Practice pronouncing each of the past tense verbs with /ed/. Record a second time and listen for accuracy.

Here is another example response:

Hi Mr. Richland / this is Julia / uh / from human resource department / we have been working on filling the position we had talked about two months ago / well um / more than one hundred people sent us their resumes to apply for the job / the committee evaluated each applicant based on their qualifications and the position requirements / it took a long time to finish the review / but finally we narrowed it down to three applicants / two applicants were interviewed Wednesday / and one applicant will be interviewed on Friday / if all three pass the interview / we hope to hire all three / (10 seconds remaining)

This response is well organized and clearly delivered. This would be considered a strong response.

●→ Tips for GIVE A PROGRESS REPORT QUESTIONS

1. You may want to use your pen and paper to jot down some key words or phrases, such as names, places, times, etc.

2. Organize your response according to the pattern provided in the question prompt: tell what the situation is, what has already been done, and what still needs to be done.

3. Be aware of the components that can go into giving a progress report, including: extend a greeting; identify yourself and your position; identify the purpose of your call; give the main conclusion of your report if known; summarize the important steps that have been accomplished; summarize the important steps that have yet to be accomplished; ask the caller for advice or help; and close with emphasizing the main idea or offering to provide more details.

4. In the greeting use a salutation like *hello* or *hi* with the person's name to create an informal, friendly mood.

5. In the self-identification, you can state your name or a pretend name and your position, company, or division within the company.

6. Briefly state the reason for your call early on in order to orient the listener to the appropriate context.

7. First, explain what has been done, and then go on to tell what is yet to be done. Include main points and leave out unnecessary details.

8. Let both the words and the expression in your voice convey the appropriate message. If you are hopeful that everything will be accomplished on time, let your words and tone sound positive. If you have doubts that everything can get done in time, use words and tone that communicate the seriousness of the situation. In most business contexts you will want to sound positive, and if there are problems you will want to provide solutions for solving the problems, such as more time or resources.

9. Close by emphasizing main ideas or offering to provide more details if wanted.

10. Pause in grammatical places. Link the sounds within any single phrase. Include primary stress on each phrase, and alternate pitch between stressed and unstressed syllables. Use the appropriate tense for what has been accomplished and what will be done in the future. Pronounce past tense *-ed* endings accurately.

Give a Progress Report Practice Questions

These practice questions will help you prepare to think quickly and respond concisely to *give a progress report* questions. On the TSE® you would normally hear the questions without being able to read them. In this practice section you will be able to see the dialogues in written form. For practice you should review the visual for 15 seconds, and then read the dialogue and think about it for 45 seconds before answering. Feel free to write down a few notes during your preparation time, but do not try to write down everything you want to say. Work on one practice question at a time. If you preview all the questions at once, you will ruin the spontaneity. Make your practice as realistic as possible by not looking ahead at other questions and by keeping to the time limit. For each question, record your responses. Then listen to each response to see if you have responded to all parts of the question in an organized manner. Correct and repeat responses that need improvement.

Practice Question 14.1

Along with a diagram you will hear a conversation between two people. Based on that information, you will be asked to make an oral progress report as if you were leaving a voice-mail message on the telephone. Pretend that you work in the planning division of an organization that is expanding facilities. You will have the next 15 seconds to review a diagram that outlines the facilities expansion for a company. (preparation time = 15 seconds)

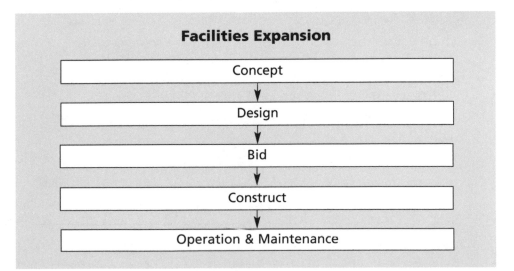

In a moment you will hear two people talking about the facility expansion. When the conversation is completed, you will have 45 seconds to prepare a voice-mail progress report for your supervisor, Ms. Witherspoon, but first listen to the conversation.

••

(On the TSE® the dialogue will be played aloud; it will not be written as it is here.)

Steve: Hi, Renee! How are the design drawings coming along for the facility expansion?

Renee: It's turned out to be more complicated than everyone thought. But we're making progress. The design drawings are complete.

Steve: Did the executive committee approve of the design yet?

Renee: Oh, yes! They were quite pleased with what we came up with, but they were a bit worried about how much it would cost.

Steve: Do you know how much it will cost?

Renee: Well our estimate was 20 percent higher than the original budget, but we're not making any changes in the design until we get all the bids in from the contractors. If the bids look reasonable, the executive committee will select one of the contractors to construct the facility. If the bids are higher than the estimate, then we may make some changes.

Steve: When will you have all the bids in?

Renee: They are due in four days, by noon Friday.

Steve: I'm anxious to hear what happens.

Renee: I'll let you know after Friday.

••

Use the next 45 seconds to prepare your report for Ms. Witherspoon. In your report be sure to:

- describe what the situation is,
- explain what has been accomplished, and
- report what is left to be done.

Do not begin your progress report voice-mail until you are instructed to do so. (preparation time = 45 seconds)

You may begin your response now. (60 seconds)

Practice Question 14.2

Along with seeing a diagram you will hear a conversation between two people. Based on that information, you will be asked to make an oral progress report as if you were leaving a voice-mail message on the telephone. Pretend that you work in the customer service division of an organization where customer orders are filled. You will have the next 15 seconds to review a diagram that outlines the process for filling customer orders. (preparation time = 15 seconds)

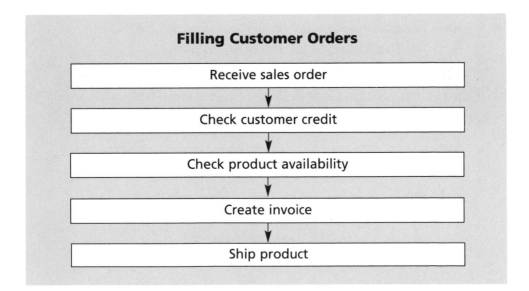

Filling Customer Orders

Receive sales order

Check customer credit

Check product availability

Create invoice

Ship product

In a moment you will hear two people talking about filling customer orders. When the conversation is completed, you will have 45 seconds to prepare a voice-mail progress report for your supervisor, Ms. Gordon, but first listen to the conversation.

••

(On the TSE® the dialogue will be played aloud; it will not be written as it is here.)

Susan: Hi, Neil! The big holiday is almost here. How are the customer orders coming?

Neil: Well, we don't have as many orders as last year, but we're still waiting on orders from our two biggest customers.

Susan: You mean Smithson and Andrews?

Neil: Yes, that's right. We always receive large orders from them around this time of year. In fact my best sales agent has been in touch with both of them, and we're expecting to receive their sales orders next week.

Susan: How is your product supply?

Neil: Sales have been up, but we have good product availability in our inventory, so within 24 hours of receiving their order we should be able to ship their requested products.

Susan: What part takes the longest in filling an order?

Neil: Well, once the sales order is received, usually checking the customer credit is the step that takes the longest.

Susan: But Smithson and Andrews both have excellent credit.

Neil: That's right, so the credit check won't delay us at all in their case.

••

Use the next 45 seconds to prepare your report for Ms. Gordon. In your report be sure to:

- describe what the situation is,
- explain what has been accomplished, and
- report what is left to be done.

Do not begin your progress report voice-mail until you are instructed to do so. (preparation time = 45 seconds)

You may begin your response now. (60 seconds)

Practice Question 14.3

Along with a diagram you will hear a conversation between two people. Based on that information, you will be asked to make an oral progress report as if you were leaving a voice-mail message on the telephone. Pretend that you work in the manufacturing division of an organization. You will have the next 15 seconds to review a diagram that outlines the production process. (preparation time = 15 seconds)

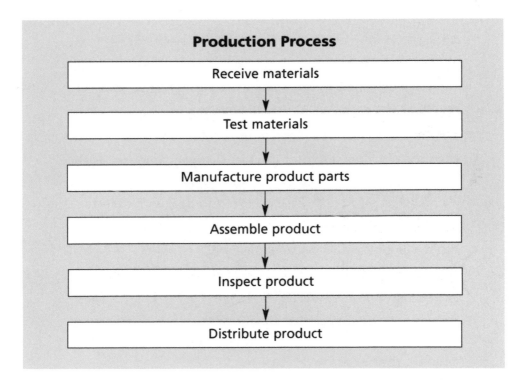

Production Process

Receive materials

↓

Test materials

↓

Manufacture product parts

↓

Assemble product

↓

Inspect product

↓

Distribute product

In a moment you will hear two people talking about the production process. When the conversation is completed, you will have 45 seconds to prepare a voice-mail progress report for your supervisor, Mr. Oglesby, but first listen to the conversation.

••

(On the TSE® the dialogue will be played aloud; it will not be written as it is here.)

Ed: Hi, Megan! How has the production process been going?

Megan: Didn't you hear? We had a big problem with quality control. Over 10 percent of assembled products were failing inspection.

Ed: That's terrible! What did you do about it?

Megan: Well, at first we thought it might be because of a problem in assembly. But that wasn't the case.

Ed: If it wasn't in assembly, where was the problem?

Megan: The problem was in the materials we were receiving from a new supplier. The materials were defective, but the materials test wasn't catching the problem.

Ed: Did you revise the materials' testing?

Megan: Yes, of course. But we also changed suppliers. Even though the materials cost a little more from this new supplier, in the long run it's cheaper than trying to deal with defective products.

Ed: Is everything running smoothly now?

Megan: Yes, we're very happy with our new supplier, and the inspection pass rate is better than ever.

••

Use the next 45 seconds to prepare your report for Mr. Oglesby. In your report be sure to:

- describe what the situation is,
- explain what has been accomplished, and
- report what is left to be done.

Do not begin your progress report voice-mail until you are instructed to do so. (preparation time = 45 seconds)

You may begin your response now. (60 seconds)

Practice Question 14.4

Along with seeing a diagram you will hear a conversation between two people. Based on that information, you will be asked to make an oral progress report as if you were leaving a voice-mail message on the telephone. Pretend that you work in the editorial division of an organization where books are prepared for publication. You will have the next 15 seconds to review a diagram that outlines the book publication process. (preparation time = 15 seconds)

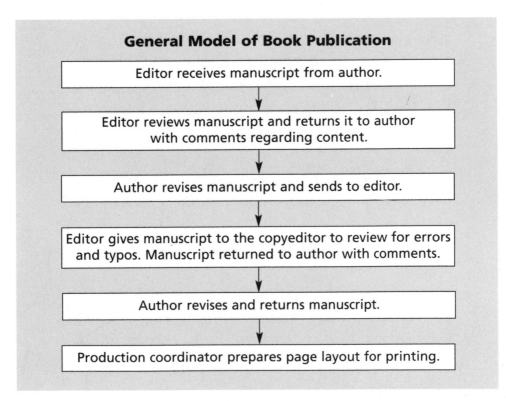

General Model of Book Publication

Editor receives manuscript from author.

Editor reviews manuscript and returns it to author with comments regarding content.

Author revises manuscript and sends to editor.

Editor gives manuscript to the copyeditor to review for errors and typos. Manuscript returned to author with comments.

Author revises and returns manuscript.

Production coordinator prepares page layout for printing.

In a moment you will hear two people talking about the publication process. When the conversation is completed, you will have 45 seconds to prepare a voice-mail progress report for your supervisor, Ms. Griffith, but first listen to the conversation.

•••

(On the TSE® the dialogue will be played aloud; it will not be written as it is here.)

Tina: Hey, Keith, what's up?

Keith: I'm editing three books right now. Two are in the copyediting stage, and the third is almost ready for printing.

Tina: That's terrific! I thought you were short on staff?

Keith: We were. One of our copyeditors was in a bad car accident and is expected to be out for six months. But we were able to hire our summer intern Mandy full time, and she's turned out to be a fantastic copyeditor.

Tina: That doesn't surprise me. She really excelled on her summer project. I'm glad to hear you were able to hire her.

Keith: The only problem I have now is with laying out that third book. There are so many figures and tables that my production coordinator is having an awful time trying to integrate it all with the text.

Tina: That does sound like a challenge.

Keith: It is, but at least the other two won't be as hard as this one.

Tina: Well, I'm sure you'll meet your deadline, Keith; you always do.

Keith: Thanks for your confidence, Tina.

•••

Use the next 45 seconds to prepare your report for Ms. Griffith. In your report be sure to:

- describe what the situation is,
- explain what has been accomplished, and
- report what is left to be done.

Do not begin your progress report voice-mail until you are instructed to do so. (preparation time = 45 seconds)

You may begin your response now. (60 seconds)

Practice Question 14.5

Along with seeing a diagram you will hear a conversation between two people. Based on that information, you will be asked to make an oral progress report as if you were leaving a voice-mail message on the telephone. Pretend that you work in the placement office of an institution. You will have the next 15 seconds to review a diagram that outlines the resume writing workshop. (preparation time = 15 seconds)

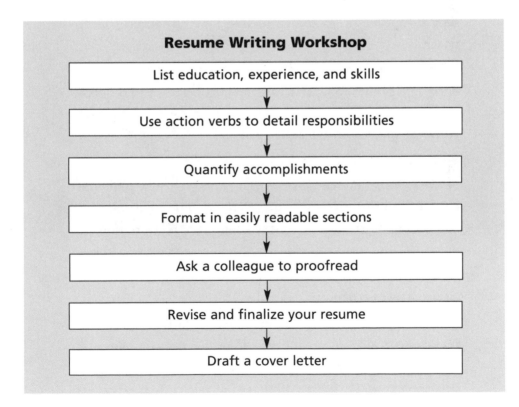

In a moment you will hear two people talking about the resume writing process. You will be asked to summarize the
status of the resume workshop to the placement office director, Mr. Hopkins, but first listen to the conversation.

••

(On the TSE® the dialogue will be played aloud; it will not
be written as it is here.)

Barry: Hi, Sandra! I passed the seminar room this morning
and saw you teaching to a packed crowd. What was going on?

Sandra: That was my workshop on resume writing. This group
was one of the most receptive I've taught in a long time.

Barry: That's good to hear. What kinds of things did you cover?

Sandra: Well, I asked all of them to come with a list of educational experiences, job experiences, and work skills.

Barry: That was a good idea to save time. What did you do
next?

Sandra: I showed them examples that highlighted the difference between using weak and strong action verbs to describe
their experiences. Then I asked them to write out their own
work experiences with action verbs.

Barry: Were they able to do that?

Sandra: Yes, they caught on real fast. The next part was
more difficult for them though. Working with a partner they
had to help each other quantify their work contribution: so
many dollars saved, so many customers served. You know,
things like that.

Barry: It sounds like you did a lot.

Sandra: For homework I asked them to format a draft of
their resume and to bring three copies that we can peer edit
at part two of the workshop next week.

••

Use the next 45 seconds to prepare your report for Mr.
Hopkins. In your report be sure to:

- describe what the situation is,
- explain what has been accomplished, and
- report what is left to be done.

Do not begin your progress report voice-mail until you are instructed to do so. (preparation time = 45 seconds)

You may begin your response now. (60 seconds)

Practice Question 14.6

Along with seeing a diagram you will hear a conversation between two people. Based on that information, you will be asked to make an oral progress report as if you were leaving a voice-mail message on the telephone. Pretend that you work as a teaching assistant for a large university course. You will have the next 15 seconds to review a diagram that outlines the process for team building. (preparation time = 15 seconds)

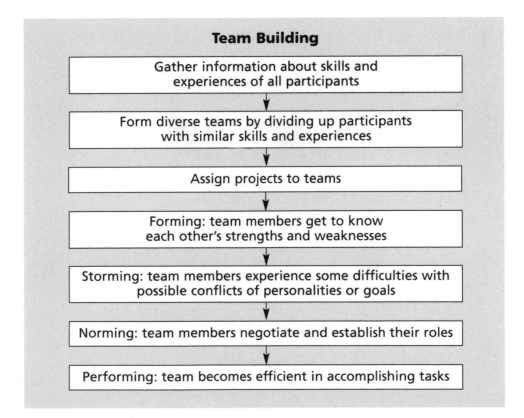

Team Building

Gather information about skills and experiences of all participants

Form diverse teams by dividing up participants with similar skills and experiences

Assign projects to teams

Forming: team members get to know each other's strengths and weaknesses

Storming: team members experience some difficulties with possible conflicts of personalities or goals

Norming: team members negotiate and establish their roles

Performing: team becomes efficient in accomplishing tasks

In a moment you will hear two teaching assistants talking about the teams in one of the classes they teach. You will be asked to summarize the status of the team work to the course supervisor, Ms. Walters, but first listen to the conversation.

••

(On the TSE® the dialogue will be played aloud; it will not be written as it is here.)

Laurel: Hey, Allan! Don't you teach on Tuesdays?

Allan: I've got class in 15 minutes. Today the student teams are presenting an update on their projects.

Laurel: I taught that class last semester. At that time there were a lot of problems with team members not getting along.

Allan: I'm really pleased with how we formed the teams. The first day of class we collected some information about each of the students and used this to create diverse teams. Each team has someone who is good with spreadsheets, someone else who is good with writing, and someone else who is good with research.

Laurel: So, are the teams working well together?

Allan: Well, things started smoothly. We assigned some easy group tasks as getting-acquainted activities that helped team members get to know each other. But things got a little rough after that.

Laurel: Rough? What do you mean by that?

Allan: In three of the five groups there were people with strong opinions and students were arguing a lot over who was in charge and how to do things. This was the classical "storming" phase. We gave the groups some training on the phases of group work, and that really helped the groups come together. The groups are in the "norming" phase now.

Laurel: That was smart to introduce some training in group dynamics. I wish we would've done that last year.

Allan: Yeah, I think I'm going to recommend to the department that group training become a regular part of the curriculum from now on.

....

Use the next 45 seconds to prepare your report for Ms. Walters. In your report be sure to:

- describe what the situation is,
- explain what has been accomplished, and
- report what is left to be done.

Do not begin your progress report voice-mail until you are instructed to do so. (preparation time = 45 seconds)

You may begin your response now. (60 seconds)

Practice Question 14.7

Along with seeing a diagram you will hear a conversation between two people. Based on that information, you will be asked to make an oral progress report as if you were leaving a voice-mail message on the telephone. Pretend that you work in an academic department of a university which has a graduate program. You will have the next 15 seconds to review a diagram that outlines the process for obtaining a graduate degree. (preparation time = 45 seconds)

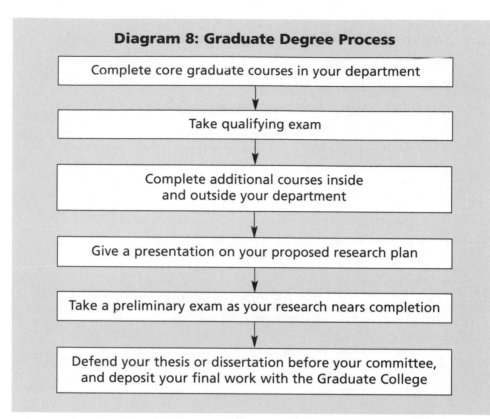

Diagram 8: Graduate Degree Process

Complete core graduate courses in your department

Take qualifying exam

Complete additional courses inside
and outside your department

Give a presentation on your proposed research plan

Take a preliminary exam as your research nears completion

Defend your thesis or dissertation before your committee,
and deposit your final work with the Graduate College

In a moment you will hear two students talking about the graduate degree process. You will be asked to summarize Raymond's progress for degree completion to a new faculty member, Ms. Welch, but first listen to the conversation.

••

(On the TSE® the dialogue will be played aloud; it will not be written as it is here.)

Nicole: Hi, Raymond. I haven't talked with you much this semester since we're not in any of the same classes.

Raymond: Actually, I'm done with my coursework now. Remember, last semester I presented my proposed research plan?

Nicole: Oh, yeah, that's right. So did your committee approve your plan?

Raymond: They approved it with some minor revisions, but their suggestions were really helpful.

Nicole: Have you started collecting data yet?

Raymond: I only took a few days off during winter break and used the rest of the time to set up my experiments. I've been able to collect a lot of data already.

Nicole: When do you think you'll take your prelim?

Raymond: I hope to take it at the beginning of next semester.

Nicole: Wow, that would be fast!

Raymond: I know it's ambitious, but if things keep going as smoothly as they are now I think I can do it.

....

Use the next 45 seconds to prepare your report for Ms. Welch. In your report be sure to:

- describe what the situation is,
- explain what has been accomplished, and
- report what is left to be done.

Do not begin your progress report voice-mail until you are instructed to do so. (preparation time = 45 seconds)

You may begin your response now. (60 seconds)

–15–

Final Notes and Test Registration Information

If you have worked your way to this point in this book, you have done some of the best preparation possible to maximize your performance on the TSE®. You are now familiar with test instructions, sample questions, time allotments, and the qualities that make good answers. Take advantage of the practice questions included at the end of each chapter. Sit down and record your answers to the practice questions in the time allotted for that type of question. Listen to your answers, and check to see how well you do in comparison to the criteria discussed in this book. Practice until you are comfortable answering new questions in a fluent, coherent, comprehensible manner. Of course, actually speaking with native speakers of American English on a regular basis is a great way to improve your communication skills.

Health, stress, environment, and other factors can have an effect on your final test performance as well. Here are some general guidelines for taking tests. Many of these suggestions came from the Counseling Center at the University of Illinois.

➡ Tips: BEFORE THE TEST

1. Get a good night's sleep.
2. Avoid taking stimulants to keep you up late the night before the test.
3. Allow ample time to get to the test site. If you don't know where the test site is, locate it prior to the test date.
4. Bring a magazine or book to read to keep you relaxed while you wait to be seated in the exam room.

5. Be positive about the test. Visualize yourself competently answering each question. Push negative thoughts aside.

6. Ask the test proctor any questions you have before the test actually begins.

7. Don't wear noisy jewelry that could make distracting noises on your test recording.

8. Prepare for the test well in advance with this book and by speaking English as much as possible. Avoid cramming the night before the test.

➡ Tips: DURING THE TEST

9. Give your complete attention to each question. Don't become distracted by noise or other examinees.

10. Sit up straight during the test in order to breathe enough air to speak clearly.

11. Talk clearly into the microphone. Don't eat candy or put other things in your mouth that could detract from your speech. Keep your hands away from your mouth and face so you can be clearly recorded.

12. Listen and read instructions carefully.

13. If you have prepared well for each type of question, you will have a good feel for how much you can say in the time allotted. However, if you get nervous about time, bring a watch with a second hand or a digital watch that counts seconds in order to pace yourself through the test. Do not bring cell phones or recording devices with you to the exam.

14. If there are any problems at all with the test equipment, notify the test proctor immediately.

15. Don't leave any question unanswered. If you don't hear a question clearly, be sure to read it in the test book. If you are unsure of the meaning of a specific question, say so. Explain how you interpret the question and answer as best as you possibly can. Raters will rate the speech sample provided as best they can. If there is no answer given or the simple response of *I don't know* or *I don't understand,* then that response will not receive many points.

16. Focus on performing the language functions required in each question, like narrating a story, sharing an opinion, or describing a graph.

●→ Tips: AFTER THE TEST

17. Don't dwell on the details of the test; this may produce more anxiety for you.
18. Reward yourself by doing something you enjoy.
19. Remember, test scores do not set a value on your personal worth!

Test Registration Information

TSE® Test

In addition to the TSE® (Test of Spoken English), Educational Testing Service (ETS) offers other oral English tests, including TOEIC® (Test of English for International Communication), and TAST® (TOEFL Academic Speaking Test). Many interviews and teaching performance tests have been developed by individual institutions for local use as well. Oral English tests serve a variety of purposes, such as placement into English programs, evaluation of progress and ability, entrance into academic or employment positions, and certification and licensing. The TSE® is an oral English test for academic and professional settings. The TOEIC® is an oral English test of everyday language in international work environments. The TAST® is an oral English test that utilizes academic contexts. The TAST® may be offered with or without the TOEFL® (Test of English as a Foreign Language). Organizations choose to utilize a particular test for a variety of reasons.

Information about these tests, such as test dates and registration forms, is distributed by ETS in various bulletins as well as on their website. ETS bulletins are frequently available at universities in the United States through the International Student centers or ESL offices on campuses. To request current test information, contact Educational Testing Service:

Educational Testing Service
Rosedale Road
Princeton, NJ 08541-6151 USA
(609) 921-9000

The websites and e-mail addresses for specific tests are provided.

Test	Website	E-mail
TSE	http://www.ets.org/tse/	ell@ets.org
TOEIC	http://www.ets.org/toeic/	toeic@ets.org
TAST	http://www.ets.org/tast/	tast@ets.org
TOEFL	http://www.ets.org/toefl/	toefl@ets.org

The phone number at ETS to inquire about the TSE is:

1-877-863-3546 (inside the U.S.)

1-609-771-7100 (outside the U.S.)

SPEAK®

SPEAK® tests are given at many universities in the United States. Sometimes the SPEAK® test is referred to as the retired TSE® since ETS created SPEAK® from TSE tests. Contact your academic department to find out who to talk to about the SPEAK® testing program on your campus.

–16–

Practice Tests

Each of the two practice tests in this chapter are similar to the TSE® test. After completing this book, use these two tests for realistic practice of an entire test. Record yourself and monitor your time. Evaluate your responses alone or with a friend based on the criteria of language function, coherence and cohesion, appropriacy, and accuracy as discussed in this book.

— Practice Test 1 —

(ID# = 28-3967)

This test is designed to help you practice for the TSE® test. Record your answer to each response. Remember to speak directly into your microphone. There are time limits following each question. The test narrator will let you know when to start and stop talking. Do your best to answer as well as you can within the stated time limit. The total test time will be about 20 minutes. These questions are not intended to measure your knowledge of any particular field, but to provide a context so that your communicative ability can be evaluated.

The next few questions are given as a warm-up. They ask simple questions about you. Do your best to give complete answers to each of these questions.

    1. What is the identification number of this test? (10 seconds)
    2. When did you begin studying English? (10 seconds)
    3. Why are you taking this test today? (10 seconds)

That completes the warm-up questions section, and now the actual test begins. For each question, try to be as clear as possible and to respond as completely as you can.

In this section of the test, you will see six pictures that depict a story line. You will be given 60 seconds to review the pictures. After that, you will be asked to tell the short story that is illustrated by the pictures. Try to include all six pictures in your story. I will let you know when to begin telling the story. (preparation time = 60 seconds)

1. Here are six pictures that illustrate a short story. Starting at the beginning, tell me the complete story picture by picture. (60 seconds)

2. Many national parks contain beautiful beaches and forests. Some people think that national parks should be free for all citizens of that nation. Other people think that it is good to charge entrance fees. Pretend you are talking with a friend and discuss the pros and cons of entrance fees for national parks. (60 seconds)

The next few questions will ask you about your thoughts on a number of different issues. Feel free to think for a couple seconds before you begin answering. Try to answer as thoroughly as you can in the time given for each question.

3. Tenure is an employment system that guarantees teachers employment under certain conditions. Some people think that it is good to have tenure for teachers. Other people think that tenure is problematic. Please tell me your opinion on this topic. (60 seconds)

4. If you could be a professional athlete, what type of sport would you choose to play? (60 seconds)

Here is a graph of Government Allocations to Education over one decade. You now have 15 seconds to review the graph.

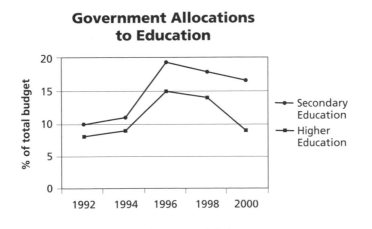

5. Please tell me about the information portrayed in this graph. (60 seconds)

6. Please propose some reasons that may explain the data shown in the graph. (60 seconds)

For the next three questions, you are to pretend that you work in a business setting or are talking with someone about business. These situations provide you with an opportunity to demonstrate how well you can converse in a business environment. Your response should be suitable for addressing the people and context provided in the situation of each question. You may find it helpful to take notes as you listen.

7. In this situation you will be asked to talk with a colleague. Pretend that your colleague has just recently received her medical license. Greet your colleague and be sure to:

   - say something about the new medical license,
   - say something positive regarding the new medical license, and
   - offer appropriate wishes to the colleague.

   Use the next 30 seconds to prepare your response. I will indicate when you should begin speaking. (preparation time = 30 seconds)

   You may begin your response now. (60 seconds)

8. In this situation you will hear and respond to a telephone message containing a complaint. Pretend that you are the manager of the kitchen in a hospital. After the message is played you will have 30 seconds to think about a response. Your response should:

   - demonstrate that you understand the caller's problem, and
   - suggest a solution to the problem that would satisfy the caller.

Please listen to the voice message. (On the TSE® the voice message will be played aloud. It will not be written as it is here.)

••

Hello. This is Gayle Hughes. I'm an RN in the east wing. I'm calling about the lunches. The lunches have been extra good this week, but they have been arriving to the rooms more than an hour late. Many of our patients are on medications that they need to take with their meals. It is really throwing off our medication schedule to have the lunches arriving so late. It's also delaying our afternoon routines and tests. I'm hoping that you can get the lunches up here on time. Please call me back this morning and let me know what you can do. I'll be at extension 7004. Thanks.

••

(The text in this box is what you will hear and is not written in the test booklet.)

You may now take 30 seconds to think about your response to the caller. I will tell you when you can start recording your response. (preparation time = 30 seconds)

Please begin your response now. (60 seconds)

9. Along with a diagram you will hear a conversation between two people. Based on that information, you will be asked to make an oral progress report as if you were leaving a voice-mail message on the telephone. Pretend that you work in a department of an organization that is hosting a conference. You will have the next 15 seconds to review a diagram that outlines the process for creating a registration system. (preparation time = 15 seconds)

Creating a Registration System

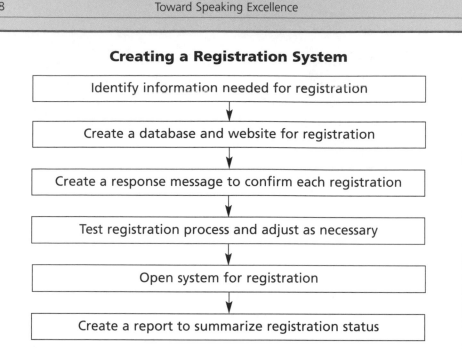

Identify information needed for registration

Create a database and website for registration

Create a response message to confirm each registration

Test registration process and adjust as necessary

Open system for registration

Create a report to summarize registration status

In a moment you will hear two people talking about the process of creating a registration system for a conference. You will be asked to summarize the status of the work to the department chair, Mr. Overton, but first listen to the conversation.

••

(On the TSE® the dialogue will be played aloud; it will not be written as it is here.)

Miguel: Hi, Angela.

Angela: Hi, Miguel. I heard you were put in charge of developing the conference registration system.

Miguel: More than 1,000 people register for the conference, so we decided to develop a Web-based registration system. I thought it would be easy, but it's taken longer than I expected.

Angela: What's been the hang-up?

Miguel: The first thing I needed to know is what information was needed for registration. Well the conference committee only meets once a month, so I waited forever to get a simple answer from them.

Angela: Is the system up and running yet?

Miguel: The database and the Web interface are designed, and I'm still waiting for approval from the committee on the confirmation response that is sent out to each registrant.

Angela: Will the system be ready in time?

Miguel: Yeah, we shouldn't have any problem making the deadline now. I'm piloting the system this week, and it should be on-line ahead of schedule.

Angela: I'm looking forward to the conference. A lot of my colleagues are coming to town for it. I'm sure they'll appreciate the on-line registration system you created.

••

Use the next 45 seconds to prepare your report for Mr. Overton. In your report be sure to:

  • describe what the situation is,
  • explain what has been accomplished, and
  • report what is left to be done.

Do not begin your progress report voice-mail until you are instructed to do so. (preparation time = 45 seconds)

You may begin your response now. (60 seconds)

End of test

— Practice Test 2 —

(ID# = 42-5159)

This test is designed to help you practice for the TSE® test. Record your answer to each response. Remember to speak directly into your microphone. There are time limits following each question. The test narrator will let you know when to start and stop talking. Do your best to answer as well as you can within the stated time limit. The total test time will be about 20 minutes. These questions are not intended to measure your knowledge of any particular field, but to provide a context so that your communicative ability can be evaluated.

The next few questions are given as a warm-up. They ask simple questions about you. Do your best to give complete answers to each of these questions.

1. What is the identification number of this test? (10 seconds)
2. When did you begin studying English? (10 seconds)
3. Why are you taking this test today? (10 seconds)

That completes the warm-up question section, and now the actual test begins. For each question, try to be as clear as possible and to respond as completely as you can.

In this section of the test, you will see six pictures that depict a story line. You will be given 60 seconds to review the pictures. After that, you will be asked to tell the short story that is illustrated by the pictures. Try to include all six pictures in your story. I will let you know when to begin telling the story. (preparation time = 60 seconds)

1. Here are six pictures that illustrate a short story. Starting at the beginning, tell me the complete story picture by picture. (60 seconds)

2. The federal governments of many countries operate post offices. Some people have suggested that private industry should take over the delivery of letters and packages. Pretend you are talking with your supervisor and discuss the pros and cons of private industry operating mail service in a country. (60 seconds)

The next few questions will ask you about your thoughts on a number of different issues. Feel free to think for a couple seconds before you begin answering. Try to answer as thoroughly as you can in the time given for each question.

3. Some people think that watching TV is a good way to learn a second language. Other people think that TV is not very helpful for language learning. I'd like to know what you think about this issue. (60 seconds)

4. If you could hire an office assistant to help in your business, what kind of qualities would you look for? (60 seconds)

Here is a graph of Road Construction over three decades. You now have 15 seconds to review the graph. (preparation time = 15 seconds)

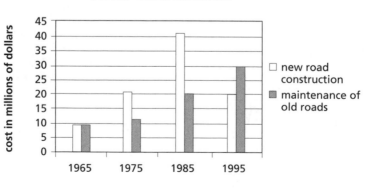

Road Construction

5. Please tell me about the information portrayed in this graph. (60 seconds)

6. Please propose some reasons that may explain the data shown in the graph. (60 seconds)

For the next three questions, you are to pretend that you work in a business setting or are talking with someone about business. These situations provide you with an opportunity to demonstrate how well you can converse in a business environment. Your response should be suitable for addressing the people and context provided in the situation of each question. You may find it helpful to take notes as you listen.

7. In this situation you will be asked to talk with a co-worker. Pretend that your co-worker has just recently received the employee-of-the-year award. Greet your co-worker and be sure to:

   • say something about the employee-of-the-year award,
   • say something positive regarding the employee-of-the-year award, and
   • offer appropriate wishes to the co-worker.

   Use the next 30 seconds to prepare your response. I will indicate when you should begin speaking. (preparation time = 30 seconds)

   You may begin your response now. (60 seconds)

8. In this situation you will hear and respond to a telephone message containing a complaint. Pretend that you are the manager of an auto parts distribution center. After the message is played, you will have 30 seconds to think about a response. Your response should:

   • demonstrate that you understand the caller's problem, and

- suggest a solution to the problem that would satisfy the caller.

Please listen to the voice message. (On the TSE® the voice message will be played aloud. It will not be written as it is here.)

••

Hello. This is Frank Cleary. I run the auto repair shop in Williamsport. We were supposed to receive a shipment of parts last Friday. It's already Tuesday, and nothing has come yet. I've got half a dozen vehicles here in my shop that are ready to go once the parts come in. I also sent back a bunch of defective hoses and belts that came in the shipment two weeks ago. This never used to happen with you guys. I called yesterday and left a message. I need to hear back from you today on this. Call me at the shop, I'll be here all day.

••

You may now take 30 seconds to think about your response to the caller. I will tell you when you can start recording your response. (preparation time = 30 seconds)

Please begin your response now. (60 seconds)

9. Along with seeing a diagram you will hear a conversation between two people. Based on that information, you will be asked to make an oral progress report as if you were leaving a voice-mail message on the telephone. Pretend that you work in the Dean's office of a university. You will have the next 15 seconds to review a diagram that outlines the procedure for filing a grievance (racial, sexual, religious harassment or discrimination, etc.). (preparation time = 15 seconds)

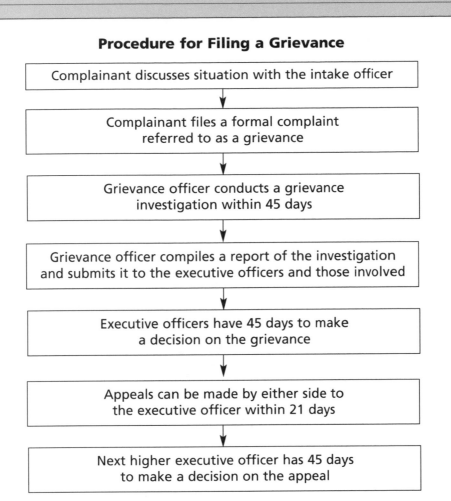

Procedure for Filing a Grievance

Complainant discusses situation with the intake officer

↓

Complainant files a formal complaint
referred to as a grievance

↓

Grievance officer conducts a grievance
investigation within 45 days

↓

Grievance officer compiles a report of the investigation
and submits it to the executive officers and those involved

↓

Executive officers have 45 days to make
a decision on the grievance

↓

Appeals can be made by either side to
the executive officer within 21 days

↓

Next higher executive officer has 45 days
to make a decision on the appeal

In a moment you will hear two grievance officers talking about a current grievance. You will be asked to summarize the status of the recent grievance to the director of the grievance office, Ms. Miller, but first listen to the conversation.

••

(On the TSE® the dialogue will be played aloud; it will not be written as it is here.)

Evan: Hi, Karla. How's it going?

Karla: Hi, Evan. It's been really busy. I've met with three complainants this month already.

Evan: That's pretty unusual.

Karla: It sure is. But it just so happens that all three were complaining about the same instructor.

Evan: Have any of them filed a formal complaint?

Karla: Oh yes, one filed a complaint and the other two are supplying additional evidence.

Evan: Do you have other witnesses to interview?

Karla: There were two and I met with them yesterday. I've also met with the grievant again and the respondent.

Evan: It sounds like you're ready to write your report.

Karla: I've started writing it. I should be able to send it to the executive officer by Friday.

•••

Use the next 45 seconds to prepare your report for Ms. Miller. In your report be sure to:

- describe what the situation is,
- explain what has been accomplished, and
- report what is left to be done.

Do not begin your progress report voice-mail until you are instructed to do so. (preparation time = 45 seconds)

You may begin your response now. (60 seconds)

End of test

— PART 3 —

The SPEAK® Test

–17–

Recommending, Giving Directions, and Describing Questions for the SPEAK® Test

In this chapter you will:

- Become familiar with the instructions for SPEAK® (the TSE® prior to 2004) questions on *recommending, giving directions,* and *describing.*
- See examples of *recommending, giving directions,* and *describing* questions and corresponding responses.
- Learn what makes an effective response to *recommending, giving directions,* and *describing* questions.
- Practice responding to a variety of *recommending, giving directions,* and *describing* questions

The general directions for the map section of the test will be something like this:

That finishes the warm-up questions and now the actual test is beginning. For each question, try to be as clear as possible and to respond as completely as you can.

> **For the next few questions try to pretend that we are classmates from college. We are looking at a map of your hometown together. Please look over the map for the next half of a minute. After that you will be asked some questions.**

In this section you will be shown a map that will be used as the context for the next three questions. Pay close attention to the context. Is the map of a place that is supposed to be new to you, or is it supposed to be of a place you are familiar with like your hometown? Are you speaking to someone who has been to this place before or is it new to them? What is your relationship to the person you are speaking with? Should you speak in a formal or informal manner? It is important to evaluate the context in order to score well on the appropriacy of your language.

You will be given 30 seconds to study the map. Use this time wisely. During those 30 seconds you should look over the names of the streets, buildings, and other landmarks. Practice pronouncing those names that look difficult to you. Generally longer words and words with consonant clusters will be more challenging to pronounce.

There are a number of common themes for street names that are used throughout cities in the United States. These themes include numbers, presidents, states, and trees. English has a number of words that are used in formal street names besides the ending *Street*. These include *Road, Avenue, Drive, Way, Boulevard, Circle*, and *Court*. The primary stress on street names depends on whether it has the ending *Street* or not. Street names with the ending *Street* carry primary stress on the word before *Street* (see Hahn and Dickerson 1998). In the following street names the underlined word carries the primary stress: <u>First</u> Street, <u>Washi</u>ngton Street, and <u>Oak</u> Street. For street names using endings other than *Street*, the primary stress goes on the ending. For example, in the following street names the underlined word carries the primary stress: Fifth <u>Av</u>enue, Wilson <u>Road</u>, and Riverside <u>Drive</u>.

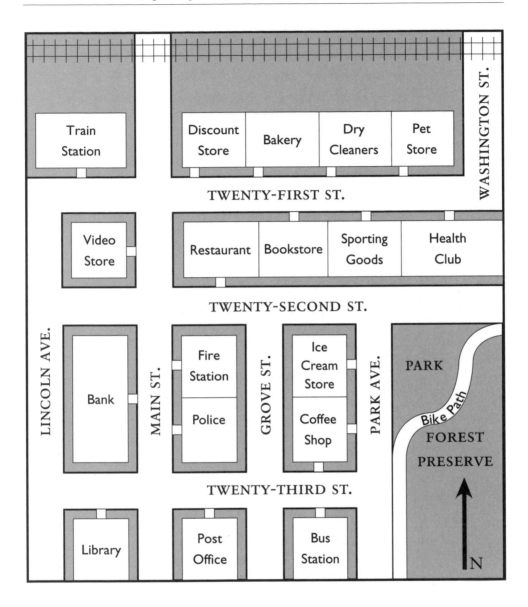

⑤ Exercise 17.1: Pronouncing Street Names

Various lists of street names are shown. It is useful to practice pronouncing some street names before the test. Look at a map of your own town or a town you plan to visit in the United States, and find three additional street names to add to each of the lists. Practice saying each of the street names from the list aloud. Look back over the list and put a check mark by the ten street names that are hardest for you to pronounce. Repeat these ten aloud for extra practice, and ask a native speaker of English to listen and correct your pronunciation if necessary.

Number streets generally use ordinal numbers like:

First Street
Second Street
Third Street
Fourth Street
Tenth Street
Twentieth Street
Twenty-first Street

_____

_____

_____

Common presidential streets include:

Washington Street
Lincoln Avenue
Jefferson Street
Roosevelt Road
Wilson Road

_____

_____

_____

Common state streets include:

Ohio Street
Illinois Street
California Street
Pennsylvania Avenue

_____

_____

_____

Common tree streets include:

Oak Street
Elm Street
Pine Street
Maple Street

_____

_____

_____

Other common U.S. street names include:

State Street
Main Street
Prospect Avenue
Franklin Road
Park Avenue
Riverside Drive

_____

_____

_____

During your time to study the map, also observe the compass directions of north, south, east, and west. Notice if there are any rivers, lakes, parks, and railroad tracks. Then look over the map and pick one place that you are familiar with and could talk about. Think of vocabulary that is associated with that place. For example, if you pick the Post Office, think of vocabulary that would be useful in describing it, like: stamps, letters, packages, long lines, overnight express, mail, ship, send, and deliver.

Exercise 17.2: Generating Terms about Places

For each of the places listed, list between five to ten words or phrases related to that type of place. Remember to include nouns, verbs, adjectives, and adverbs if possible.

Library	Bank	Book Store

Health Club	Pet Store	Discount Store
_____	_____	_____
_____	_____	_____
_____	_____	_____
_____	_____	_____
_____	_____	_____
_____	_____	_____
_____	_____	_____
_____	_____	_____
_____	_____	_____
_____	_____	_____

Recommend Questions

The *recommend* question may be something like:

> **Imagine that we are classmates from college. I came to visit you at home during break, but you got sick after I arrived. Suggest one place in town you think I should go on my own and explain the reasons why you recommend this place.** (30 seconds)

Although only 30 seconds is allotted for the answer of this question, it is wise to take a couple of seconds to organize your thoughts. Since this sample question asks you to give reasons, try to give more than one reason. For example, if you chose the Ice Cream Shop, you might mention the large variety of flavors, the natural ingredients, and the low prices. Don't try to think of too many reasons because you will either waste time or rush to say everything you want to say. On the other hand, if you can only think of one reason, that is alright as long as you clearly explain your one reason. Frame your response in a way that will help the rater to understand what you say; this includes previewing your reasons, providing details, and concluding. Speaking in this manner communicates that you are a clear thinker with the ability to communicate your thoughts in words. In other words, it sounds like you are in control of your language rather than just speaking haphazardly off the top of your head. Furthermore, because you have a solid strategy to answer questions, you can speak more confidently. Here is a sample response:

> *I think you really ought to go to the Ice Cream Store. I know you'll enjoy it for three important reasons!*
>
> *First of all they have a variety of flavors, over 100 different kinds! Second, all their ice cream is made with natural ingredients. No preservatives or artificial flavors are used. But best of all are the low prices!*
>
> *I know you like a choice of healthy, inexpensive treats, so the Ice Cream Store is definitely a place you'll want to go!*

The exclamation marks point out the need to speak enthusiastically. Since you have been asked to role-play, you want your recommendation to sound convincing. Enthusiasm will help you put the needed intonation in your voice. Enthusiasm also tends to lower your anxiety level, which in turn lets you communicate to your maximum potential.

Since this context stages two college classmates talking, informal language is appropriate. Notice the use of contractions like *you'll*. Also notice the familiarity expressed in phrases like *I think you really ought to, I know you'll enjoy it,* and *I know you like a*. Rhythm can also be enhanced by using reduced forms like *oughta* for *ought to* and *wanna* for *want to*.

The previous answer is divided into three parts: preview, details, and conclusion. The preview is just two short sentences. Its purpose is to introduce the topic and clue the rater about what to listen for. The topic is clearly the Ice Cream Shop, and the rater is guided to listen for three key reasons. U.S. listeners expect to be guided in their listening in this way. So if you don't guide your rater like this, you will make him or her work harder to understand you.

The middle four sentences give the details one by one. Transitions and markers are used to highlight the key ideas: *First of all, Second,* and *But best of all.* Details are given to make the ideas concrete. Variety is described as *over 100 different kinds,* and natural ingredients is explained as *no preservatives or artificial flavors.* The response time is short, so avoid talking about ideas that are abstract because abstract ideas are hard to describe and explain.

The conclusion is only one sentence in this example answer, but it is an important part of the answer because it summarizes the main ideas with the words *choice, healthy,* and *inexpensive.* At the end of the allotted response time, you will hear the narrator say the number of the next test question followed by directions for the next question. If you keep speaking about your reasons until after the narrator goes on to the next question, it might sound as if you don't know how to concisely answer the question. If you do run out of time, rather than stop mid-sentence, finish your sentence, but don't say more than a few words after the response time has ended. However, by including a short summary within the allotted time, you demonstrate that you are in control of your thoughts and your language. The summary keeps the main ideas in the rater's mind, so the raters find it easier to recall your main points and thereby conclude you have accomplished the intended language function. This gives a positive impression of your communication skills.

One common mistake made by test-takers is to merely give a list of places to go, as was done in the following response.

> *It would be nice to go to the Ice Cream Shop, or you might want to go to the Discount Store, or the Bakery is nearby, or the Book Store. The Sporting Goods Store is another place or the Health Club next door. The other place you could go is the Library.*

This type of response, even if spoken fluently, will be scored low because it does not give any reasons for visiting any of these places.

⑤ Exercise 17.3: Generating Ideas about Places

This exercise is for additional practice on generating ideas quickly about different places. Place a check mark by one of the five places listed, and write a short paragraph about it. After writing your paragraph, close your book and describe the same place aloud in order to work on fluency.

_____ a crowded supermarket

_____ a picnic in the mountains

_____ a championship basketball game

_____ a classroom on the day of the final exam

_____ a computer lab at a university

_____

_____

_____

_____

_____

_____

_____

_____

_____

_____

Giving Directions Questions

The *giving directions* question may be something like this:

> **I would like to pick up a movie at the video store for us to watch. Could you please give me directions from the coffee shop to the video store?** (30 seconds)

During the time given to review the map, you already noted the compass directions of north, south, east, and west. You may choose to use these compass directions, or you may say *up, down, left,* and *right.* Whichever form of directions you choose, be consistent. Don't switch back and forth from north to up to east, etc. If you identified any street names that you don't feel confident in pronouncing, try to avoid them if possible. Otherwise, pronounce them slowly to enunciate each syllable of each problem word. For distance on a city map you can use the term *blocks.* Since you need a few seconds to find these two places on the map, don't expect to talk for the whole 30 seconds. Remember your role, the context, and your relationship to the speaker. You may also want to include other landmarks as you describe the way to go. Here is a sample response:

> *Exit the coffee shop onto Twenty-third Street between Park Avenue and Grove Street. Walk west on Twenty-third Street for one and a half blocks. At Twenty-third and Main, turn north. On the second block you'll see a large restaurant on the east side of the street. On the west side, across from the restaurant, is the video store.*

In this example you are talking to a classmate who has probably never been to your home town before. Referring to landmarks like *across from the restaurant* is appropriate language to employ in this context. Clear directions are important for someone who is new in town. For example, if the starting place is on a corner, be sure to specify which street you are starting on. Also look for indications of doorways or entrances to know where to start and finish. It's important not to confuse the rater from the start; therefore, it is a good idea to specify exactly where you are beginning your directions. Look for the most direct route. There are other ways to get to the Video Store from the Coffee Shop, but all of these require more streets and more turns. Some people can finish responding to this question before the 30-second time limit. If you finish the task clearly and concisely with time remaining, don't feel pressured to add more to your response because you may make mistakes or sound unorganized. A simple, concise answer will communicate clearly to the rater and will reduce the opportunity for errors and confusion.

Here is another good alternative response. Think about what makes this set of directions clear.

> *OK, you want to get from the Coffee Shop to the Video Store. From the Coffee Shop take Twenty-third Street west. Pass Grove Street and then turn right on Main Street. The first street you come to is Twenty-second Street. Crossing Twenty-second Street you will see the Video Store on the left. There's a large neon sign in the window, you can't miss it.*

⑤ Exercise 17.4: Using Pauses When Giving Directions

An important part of giving directions is using appropriate pausing. In the preceding response, put a slash (/) at each place you would pause. Now give the directions in the response out loud while using appropriate pausing. Ask a native speaker of English to give you feedback on your pausing and pace.

⬡ Exercise 17.5: Writing and Giving Directions

For additional practice, write out directions from your home to the grocery store for an older uncle who has come to visit you. Remember to use appropriate directions and landmarks. Review your directions and insert a slash (/) where you think it is appropriate to pause. Practice giving your directions aloud.

_____

_____

_____

_____

_____

_____

Describing Questions

The *describing* question may be something like this:

> **Imagine that after coming back from the Video Store you show me the title of the movie you picked out. It happens to be one of your favorite movies. Please tell me about the movie and why you find it interesting.** (60 seconds)

You may have many favorite movies; don't take a long time debating with yourself about which one you should talk about. Pick a movie that will be easy for you to talk about. This could be a movie you have seen recently so the story is fresh in your mind, or it could be a movie you enjoy a lot so it is still vivid in your memory. If you have never seen a movie, or can't remember the last time you have seen a movie, pick a favorite book to talk about and pretend that it has been made into a movie.

Notice that the question has two parts: first you are asked to talk about the movie, and then you are asked to explain why you like it. As with the recommendation question, give your answer in the form of preview, details, and conclusion. If you try to talk about the plot of the story and then give the reasons you like it, you are probably going to run out of time. Therefore, give the reasons you like the movie by giving examples from it. In that way you will be able to describe part of the movie and the reasons you like it at the same time. With this approach you are much more likely to complete your answer in the time allotted. Be sure to keep your comments short and to the point. Think of one or two reasons why you like this story; you probably won't have time to talk about more than that. Keep your reasons short, but make them concrete so they will be easily understood by the rater. If you are talking about a movie the rater has never seen and your explanation is vague and rambling, your rating will suffer.

Since this is a movie you like, be enthusiastic. In the conclusion encourage the rater to watch this movie. Remember, enthusiasm will help you put the needed intonation in your voice and will help lower your anxiety level, which in turn lets you communicate to your maximum potential. Here is an example response:

> *One of my favorite movies is "It's a Wonderful Life"! There are two main reasons why I like this fascinating story.*
>
> *The first reason I like this movie is because it shows how the decisions and actions of one person's life can affect many other lives! For example, when George was a boy he jumped into the broken ice of a pond to save his younger brother. George's brother later grew up to be a pilot in the Air Force and saved the lives of many American soldiers. If George hadn't saved his brother when he was a kid, his brother couldn't have saved those soldiers! The other reason I like this movie is because it's shown on*

> *TV every year at Christmas time. It has become like a*
> *tradition to watch it every year.*
>
> *If you haven't seen "It's a Wonderful Life," I highly*
> *recommend it. It's an interesting story that shows us how*
> *closely our lives are tied to each others'. Who knows, you*
> *may start your own tradition of watching it every year!*

This answer starts out by identifying the movie and clueing the rater that there are two key reasons for liking it. The middle part gives details about the story and the reasons for liking it. Each reason is introduced with a transition statement or marker: *The first reason* and *The other reason.* Enough details are shared to give the rater an idea of the plot, but not so many details that the speaker strays from directly answering the question. Pronouns are avoided in specific places in order to eliminate confusion. So instead of saying, *He later grew up to be a pilot,* the speaker says, *George's brother later grew up to be a pilot.* That way there is no confusion about who is the pilot. When making comparisons or contrasts make sure the primary stress reflects this focus. (See Hahn and Dickerson 1998 for more information on how to use primary stress for comparison and contrast.) For example, in this sentence the underlined words are being compared and should therefore carry primary stress. *If George hadn't saved his brother when he was a kid, his brother couldn't have saved those soldiers! George* and *brother* are being compared to *brother* and *soldiers.* Since how you say something communicates as well as what you say, be sure to place appropriate stress within a phrase. The final two sentences conclude the answer first with a brief summary and then with an encouragement to watch this movie. Notice exclamation points throughout as reminders to let your intonation show your enthusiasm for the movie. Other markers that communicate enthusiasm are expressions like *fascinating story* and *I highly recommend it.*

Another approach to answering this question would be to talk about the director or the stars rather than the plot.

This is a video of one of my favorite movies, "It's a Won-derful Life"! Both the directing and the acting in this clas-sic film are superb!

This is one of the better-known films directed by the famous director, Frank Capra. In this movie, Capra shows how a kind-hearted individual can triumph over evil in the world. Capra depicts life in small town America through the Depression and World War II in such a way that you feel like you are really living it. The acting is great too. Jimmy Stewart plays the lead role of George Bailey in such a natural way. Stewart beautifully portrays the conflict between dreams and responsibility in this part. Donna Reed also does an excellent job of starring as George's wife.

I think you will be glad that you saw this memorable movie with me.

🎦 Exercise 17.6: Describing a Movie

Now think of a movie you have seen and record yourself while you pretend to tell a friend why you did or did not like it. After recording your response, listen to your response and evaluate how well you:

- *introduced the name of the movie,*
- *clarified your opinion, whether you like or don't like this movie,*
- *used specific examples,*
- *used transitions,*
- *related your explanation to your audience, and*
- *used appropriate intonation.*

Recommending, Giving Directions, and Describing Practice Questions

These practice questions will help you prepare to think quickly and respond concisely to *recommending, giving directions,* and *describing* questions. You should study the appropriate map before answering the questions. Work on one practice set at a time. If you preview all the questions at once, you will ruin the spontaneity. Make your practice as realistic as possible by not looking ahead at other questions and by keeping the time limit. For each set of questions, record your responses. Then listen to each response to see if you have accurately responded to the specific language function, and if you have structured your answer in an easy-to-follow manner. Correct and repeat responses that need improvement.

Practice Set 1
See Map on page 251.

Imagine I am your co-worker visiting you from out of town:

- There are plans for a new fast-food restaurant to be built in town. What are some reasons a person might like to go there? (30 seconds)
- I'm getting hungry. Please tell me how to get from the park to the restaurant. (30 seconds)
- It's a sunny day and you are taking a walk in the park. Please tell me about the activities you see taking place at the park and why this park is beneficial to this town. (60 seconds)

Practice Set 2
See Map on page 251.

Imagine I am your supervisor at work and we are talking during coffee break:

- Coffee shops have become popular places. What are some of the reasons people like to go to coffee shops? (30 seconds)

- I need to buy some food for my pet. Please give me directions from the coffee shop to the pet store. (30 seconds)
- You just stopped at the pet store last night. Please tell me about an animal you think would make a good pet and why you think so. (60 seconds)

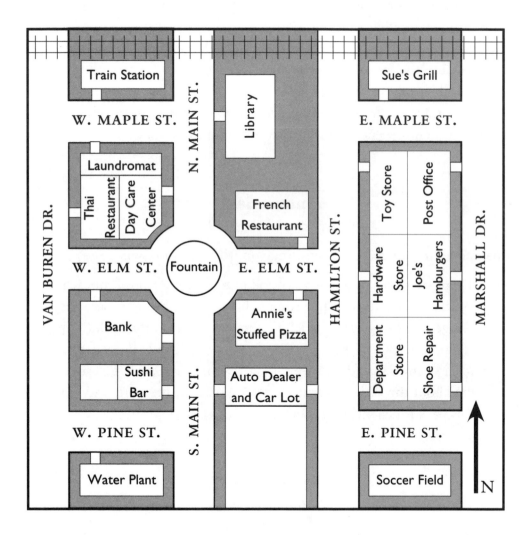

Practice Set 3

See Map on page 266.

Imagine we're classmates from college and I came for a visit in your home town:

- Because you have a soccer match, you won't be able to meet me at the train station when I arrive. So, give me directions from the train station to the soccer field. (30 seconds)
- After the soccer match we are both hungry. Suggest one of the restaurants for us to eat at and give reasons why you think it would be a good place for us to eat. (30 seconds)
- Over dinner we talk. Tell me about a recent book you've read and why you like it. (60 seconds)

Practice Set 4

See Map on page 266.

Imagine you are talking with your younger sister who is visiting from out of town:

- There is a large library in town. What are some reasons for going to a library? (30 seconds)
- I need to look at some newspapers at the library. Please tell me how to get from the post office to the library. (30 seconds)
- You just came from the library. Please tell me about your favorite newspaper or magazine and why you like it. (60 seconds)

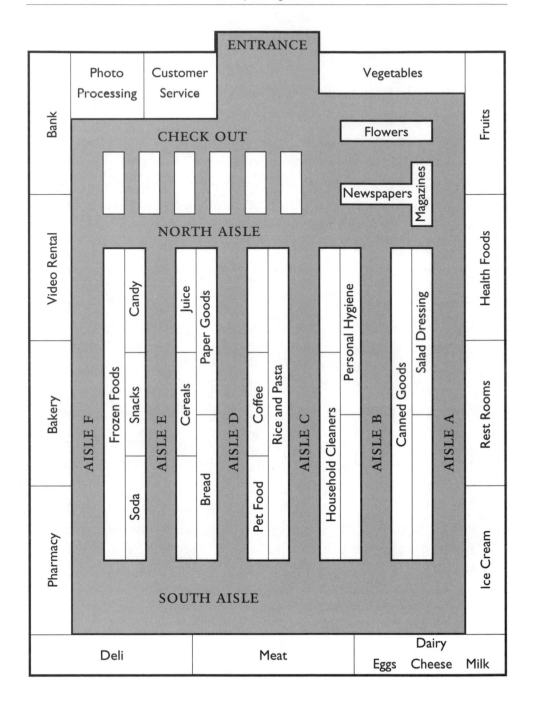

Practice Set 5

See Map on page 268.

Imagine that you work at this store and this is my first time to come here:

- I have wanted to lose some weight and just started a diet. Could you suggest some food for me to buy and tell me why you think it would be good for my diet? (30 seconds)
- I'm running late and need to pick up a few things quickly. I have just entered the store. Please give me directions from the apples to the toothpaste to the coffee. (30 seconds)
- This evening I have invited some friends over for a party. Please tell me about some food I could serve and give some reasons why you think this is good party food. (60 seconds)

Practice Set 6

See Map on page 268.

Imagine that we are neighbors and run into each other at this store:

- I'm thirsty and am trying to pick out something to drink. Recommend one beverage and tell me why you think I should buy it. (30 seconds)
- I'm not sure where to find a couple of items in the store. Please give me directions from the napkins to the sandwich meat to the carrots. (30 seconds)
- Please tell me about one of your favorite breakfast foods and why you like it. (60 seconds)

–18–

Suggest and Persuade Questions for the SPEAK® Test

In this chapter you will:

- Become familiar with the instructions for the SPEAK® (the TSE® prior to 2004) *suggest a solution* and *persuade* questions.
- See examples of *suggest a solution* and *persuade* questions and corresponding responses.
- Learn what makes an effective response to *suggest a solution* and *persuade* questions.
- Practice responding to a variety of *suggest a solution* and *persuade* questions.

The general directions for the picture section of the test may be something like this:

> **In this section of the test you will see six pictures that depict a story line. You will be given 60 seconds to review the pictures. After that you will be asked to tell the short story that is illustrated by the pictures. Try to include all six pictures in your story. When the test narrator tells you to, you may start telling the story.**

Narrating the story shown in the picture sequence is still part of the SPEAK® Test and is covered in Chapter 6. In the SPEAK®, the *narrate a story* question is generally followed by a hypothetical question about how to avoid the problem shown, and another question asking to persuade someone. Please refer to picture sequence 1 in Chapter 6 on page 63 for the following questions.

Suggest a Solution Questions

The *suggest a solution* question may be something like this:

> **What could the biker have done specifically to avoid this problem?** (30 seconds)

In the initial 60 seconds you are given to study the picture story, you should anticipate this question by first identifying the main problem or conflict and then determining ways to avoid the problem. Listen to the question carefully. If the question is in conditional form, then the answer should be in conditional form. An if-then statement is a useful way to express this. Organize your answer by first clearly stating the problem, then offering one possible solution, and then concluding. Here is a sample response:

> *The biker needs to ride more carefully to avoid getting a flat tire. If the biker had watched the path instead of gazing at the trees and lake, then the biker could have steered the bike away from the sharp rock. It does not look like there are many rocks in the path, which means that this flat tire was just an unhappy coincidence. With a little care and a little luck this problem will probably not happen again soon.*

This response starts out with a clear statement of the problem and clues the rater that a simple solution will be discussed. Then the details of the solution are given. The if-then statement clearly explains the alternative solution and the result. The possible solution is, *If the biker had watched the path instead of gazing at the trees and lake.* The result from this solution is *then the biker could have steered the bike away from the sharp rock.* Notice how details are used to clarify meaning. Instead of just saying *gazing away,* the examinee responds with the details of *at the trees and lake.* Also the appropriate tense is used in the if-then statement, *had watched* and *could have steered away.* Again, transitions are important. The transition phrase *which means that* connects the ideas of *not many rocks* and an *unhappy coincidence.*

It is not necessary to give more than one alternative solution. If you try to say too much you may rush yourself and hurt your communicative ability. Furthermore, if you try to say too much, you may not have time to fully explain your ideas, thereby hurting your communicative ability. Try to speak for at least 75 percent of the time allotted.

This response also includes a one-sentence conclusion. This conclusion emphasizes that the problem is easily avoided and leaves the rater with a clear understanding of what was trying to be communicated. Hence, the rater is left with a good impression of the communicative ability of this examinee.

One thing to avoid with this type of question is a vague response such as *"This could have been avoided if he had been more careful."* This statement can apply to almost any accident or problem, so it is not very effective in communicating your ability to suggest specific solutions to problems. One technique to overcome this problem of vagueness is to imagine that your boss is asking you to suggest solutions. It would be unacceptable to simply suggest being more careful to a problem your boss asked you to solve. Likewise it is unacceptable to give such a vague answer on the SPEAK®. Here is another alternative response to this question:

> *The bike path needs to be maintained better in order to avoid flat tires. Workers should be hired to clear the path of rocks and branches on a regular basis. It would not take a lot of effort to make the path safe for bikers.*

Persuade Questions

The *persuade* question may be something like this:

Pretend that you are the bike rider portrayed in the pictures. After you have taken the bike back to the rental booth, you find out that the cashier will not return your money. You think you deserve a refund; however, the bike rental has a policy of no refunds. After you arrive home you call the owner of the bike rental. Try to persuade the owner to refund your five-dollar rental fee. (45 seconds)

This question asks you to imagine that this situation is happening to you. In order to role-play you must take on the feelings and goals of the character and express those in English. Since you are role-playing a phone call, the first thing you need to do is to greet the person on the other end of the phone and identify yourself. Be sure to speak in present tense because you are acting out the situation, not describing a past event. Typical phone greetings are *Hello*, or *Hello, this is John Smith*. Since this is a one-sided phone conversation, you have to imagine that someone answers on the other side of the telephone. You will need to maintain the telephone call for 45 seconds without someone giving a response to your comments.

After the greeting, explain the reason you are calling which, in this case, will include what happened and why you want your money back. Say the specific amount of money you expect to be refunded so the rater knows exactly what you hope to receive. In the United States most people will be polite but firm when making this type of request over the phone. The test task is asking you to use your language ability to persuade. Rude or overly commanding behavior generally is not considered very persuasive in the United States. Stating logical reasons for why you want your request granted will usually be more persuasive than demanding something to be done. Another facet of persuading is making some concessions in order to make it easier for the other person to do what you ask. In this situation you could offer to accept a $5.00 coupon for biking rather than demand the $5.00 cash back. Here is an example response:

> *Hello, this is John Smith. Earlier today I rented a bicycle from your rental booth in the park and the bike I was riding had a flat tire. I then had to walk the bicycle back in the hot sun! This was exhausting and not much fun! You know, if you're going to be renting these bicycles, I think they should be in better condition. Furthermore, the bicycle paths need to be better maintained. There are rocks and litter all over the path, it is impossible not to hit something! So I would like to ask for my $5.00 back. . . . Well, if your policy doesn't allow refunds, at least you could give me a coupon for a free bicycle rental another day. . . . Thanks, I knew you'd understand.*

This answer starts with an appropriate telephone greeting. Since your identity as a test-taker is supposed to remain unknown to the rater, do not use your real name in the greeting. Since the name John was arbitrarily chosen for an earlier question, it was used again here so as not to confuse the raters with a name change. The last name of Smith was arbitrarily chosen as well.

The speaker quickly identifies the reason for his call: *I rented a bicycle and . . . had a flat tire.* Descriptive words like *hot sun, exhausting,* and *not much fun* are used to explain why this was an inconvenience to the customer and to encourage the owner to sympathize with the situation. To further persuade the owner, the speaker provides two reasons why the owner should take responsibility for the flat tire: The owner needs to better maintain the bicycles and the bicycle paths. Along with logical organization, transitions and connections also help to enhance the communicative power of the response. Expressions such as *Earlier today, I then had to walk, if you are going to, Furthermore, So I would like to,* and *Well, if* help the response to flow smoothly.

The speaker is successful in expressing his request while remaining polite. The request is softened or made more polite by phrases like *I think* and *I would like to ask.* Exclamation marks point out the need to speak persuasively and with passion in order to accomplish the desired goal. Additionally, U.S. speakers are frequent users of contractions in informal conversation, so a number of contractions are used, like *you're, doesn't,* and *you'd.* Contractions allow the speaker to sound fluent by maintaining the rhythm of English.

One important aspect of appropriacy of language is to call people by appropriate names. Don't just put Miss, Ms., Mrs., or Mr. in front of someone's title, like Mr. Owner, Ms. Storekeeper, Miss Supervisor, or Mrs. Professor. These expressions are never used in real life. Role-plays should sound realistic, so if necessary insert a name such as Mr. Johnson, Ms. Nelson, Miss Brown, or Professor Cole.

Brief pauses are indicated by the three dots (. . .) in the response. This makes for a more realistic role-play and makes the speaker sound more communicative. The last sentence concludes the phone conversation on a positive note. Since there is no one actually responding to you, you should assume that the owner is positively persuaded by your answer. The polite positive ending will leave the rater with a positive impression of your ability to use English to persuade others.

Here is an alternative response to this question:

Hello. May I speak with the owner of the bike rental? . . . Thanks.

Hello, Mr. Johnson? This is John Smith. I'd like to talk with you about a problem I had while renting one of your bikes in the park today. The bike I rented had a flat tire, so I had to walk the bicycle back to the rental booth in the hot sun! I spent $5.00 for a bike ride and spent most of the hour pushing the bike back! When I explained the situation to the cashier at the booth, he wasn't very helpful. This just doesn't seem fair to me! So, I would like to ask for my $5.00 back. . . . Yes, I can stop by this afternoon to pick it up. Thanks.

---

⑤ Exercise 18.1: Generating Expressions for Making Requests

Here is a short list of polite expressions for making requests. See what others you can add to the list.

> please
> could you please
> would you mind
> if you don't mind
> if it's not too much trouble
> if it's not too much of an inconvenience

_____

_____

_____

_____

⑤ Exercise 18.2: Making Polite Requests

Now choose a few of the expressions in Exercise 18.1 to make a variety of requests. After each request suggested in the phrases, write out a polite request. Then say your requests aloud.

1. borrow a book: _____

_____

_____

2. repeat that question: _____

_____

_____

3. set an appointment: _____

_____

_____

4. ask for the time: _____

_____

_____

5. ask a friend to proofread your paper: _____

_____

_____

6. ask for a ride home: _____

_____

_____

Suggest a Solution and Persuade Practice Questions

These practice questions will help you prepare to think quickly and respond concisely to *suggest a solution* and *persuade* questions. You should study the sequence of six pictures shown with each practice set before answering the questions that follow. Work on one practice set at a time. If you preview all the questions at once, you will ruin the spontaneity. Make your practice as realistic as possible by not looking ahead at other questions and by keeping the time limit. For each set of questions below, record your responses. Then listen to each response to see if you have accurately responded to the specific language function, and if you have appropriately addressed the intended audience. Correct and repeat responses that need improvement.

Practice Questions 18.1

Please refer to the practice question 6.1 picture sequence in Chapter 6 on page 75.

- What precautions could have been taken to avert this incident? (30 seconds)
- Let's pretend you are the customer who falls in this scene. Go talk to the manager of this restaurant and convince her to replace your food free of charge. (45 seconds)

Practice Questions 18.2

Please refer to the practice question 6.2 picture sequence in Chapter 6 on page 76.

- What precautions could have been taken to avert this incident? (30 seconds)
- Let's pretend that you are the person in this scene. You have an important date in about an hour, and you want to make a good impression. You need to shower and change your clothes, but you can't leave with a dirty car. Talk to your roommate and convince him or her to clean your car for you while you get yourself ready. (45 seconds)

Practice Questions 18.3

Please refer to the practice question 6.3 picture sequence in Chapter 6 on page 77.

- What precautions could have been taken to avert this incident? (30 seconds)
- Let's pretend that you are the person in this scene. Call the neighbor, who owns the dog, and convince him to buy you new flowers. (45 seconds)

Practice Questions 18.4

Please refer to the practice question 6.4 picture sequence in Chapter 6 on page 78.

- What precautions could have been taken to avert this incident? (30 seconds)
- Let's pretend you are a parent of a child with a new bicycle. The brakes on the bicycle break the first day your child uses it. You decide to take the bicycle back to the store. Persuade the bicycle store manager to replace the broken parts free of charge. (45 seconds)

Practice Questions 18.5

Please refer to the practice question 6.5 picture sequence in Chapter 6 on page 79.

- Let's pretend the customer drops the new TV as he is carrying it to his car. What precautions could have been taken to avert this accident? (30 seconds)
- Let's pretend you are the person in this scene. Although you already have a pretty good TV at home, you really want to buy this new one. Call your spouse on the phone and try to persuade him or her that you should buy this new TV set. (45 seconds)

–19–

Define or Explain Questions
for the SPEAK® Test

In this chapter you will:

- Become familiar with the instructions for the SPEAK® (the TSE® prior to 2004) *define or explain* questions.
- See examples of *define or explain* questions and corresponding responses.
- Learn what makes an effective response to *define or explain* questions.
- Practice responding to a variety of *define or explain* questions.

The general directions for the graph section may be something like this:

The next few questions will ask you about your thoughts on a number of different issues. Feel free to think for a couple seconds before you begin answering. Try to answer as thoroughly as you can in the time given for each question.

The questions in this section cover a number of topics, and each question focuses on a different function of language. This chapter focuses on the *define or explain* questions. In order to accomplish these communication goals in the small amount of time given to respond, you will need a strategy and some practice. The raters don't expect you to begin speaking immediately, so don't start speaking your response immediately after the question is given. Take a few seconds to organize your thoughts.

The *define or explain* question may be something like this:

> **Imagine you are a graduate student and a group of high school students come to visit your campus. As you give them a tour of your department, tell them about a basic topic in your area of study.** (60 seconds)

Defining a concept or term or explaining a topic is a language function you should think about and prepare for. The test may give you something specific to define or may give you the freedom to pick a concept or term of your choice within a given range of possibilities, as in the preceding sample question. Generally, it is not useful to memorize definitions, because it is too difficult to predict what you might be asked for on the test. Additionally, memorized responses tend to focus the speaker on remembering the "right words" rather than on communicating the message to a specific audience with the appropriate intonation and rhythm. Furthermore, memorizing definitions may tempt the speaker to give a memorized definition as an answer to a question where the term itself or the phrasing doesn't fit the given audience and context. Raters can generally see through memorized answers and rate them down accordingly. Nonetheless, it will help you to have practiced defining other concepts and terms ahead of time so you will have a strategy to use in defining any concept or term asked of you. The outline below is adapted from an approach for defining a term that is recommended by Smith, Meyers, and Burkhalter (1992).

1. Clearly state the concept or term you are defining.
2. Explain the importance of this concept or term.
3. Give a concise definition of the concept or term.
4. Provide examples or analogies that relate to your listeners and help clarify the concept or term.
5. Conclude your definition by emphasizing key ideas or by motivating your listeners.

With practice you can learn to apply this strategy for defining concepts and terms in order to maximize the effectiveness of your communication.

The first thing to do in responding to this question is to choose a concept. You should choose something that is very simple, because you only have one minute to define it. Since the question implies that the audience has no background in your field, try to pick a concept that most people have heard of before. In this way, as you speak the rater may recall what he or she already knows about this concept. If you choose an obscure term, then the rater may be unable to relate anything you say to his or her own knowledge or experience. Picking somewhat familiar terms or concepts is important because your communicative ability will be rated on, in part, by how well you respond to a particular audience.

Here is a sample response:

> *The topic I would like to explain for you is concrete. Concrete is a very important substance because it is a basic material for most construction projects like large buildings and airports. Concrete is composed of three parts, aggregate, cement, and water. Aggregate includes gravel and sand. Cement acts as a glue. Water is necessary to start the binding action of the cement. One way to understand concrete is to think of the candy peanut brittle. Peanuts can be compared to aggregate. Sugar and water are mixed to form a syrup that dries to hold the peanuts in peanut brittle. This is similar to the way cement and water dry to hold the aggregate in concrete. Sometimes peanut brittle gets pretty hard, but concrete is even harder. That is why concrete is an excellent material for construction.*

The topic chosen for this response was concrete. This is a good choice because most people have a general idea of what concrete is and how it is used, though they may not know how it is composed. The response begins with a clear statement that the concept to be discussed is *concrete*. It is important that the rater knows what you are defining before you go into the details of an explanation. It is also important to tell why this term is important. The second sentence of the response says that concrete is important *because it is a basic material for most construction projects* and then goes on to give specific examples of projects *like large buildings and airports*. Specific examples help the rater to better understand the ideas expressed.

Next, a formal definition of concrete is given. In this case concrete is formally defined by the parts that go together to make it, *aggregate, cement* and *water*. Cohesion is maintained by defining each of the three parts in the order they were mentioned. Long chemical names are avoided because they may be difficult to pronounce and the rater may not understand even if they are pronounced correctly. Formulas and other technical details are avoided because there is only a short time to respond and these would more than likely confuse the rater and detract from communication.

After the formal definition an analogy is given to help a non-expert understand a field-specific term. This may be the hardest part of the strategy for giving a definition, depending on the term. Generally, it takes people time to think of and develop analogies. So if an analogy does not readily come to mind, this may be something that is skipped in your definition. However, analogies are a powerful way for you to communicate to non-experts the basic ideas of your field-specific term. In this response the analogy is introduced with a transition: *One way to understand concrete.* Choose an analogy that most people are familiar with. *Peanut brittle* was chosen in this case. This is a candy most people know about. Avoid analogies to complex items because they cause you to focus on explaining the analogy rather than the concept, and in the end communication suffers. When using analogies make clear connections to your concept. In this response *peanuts* were compared with *aggregate*, and *sugar and water* were compared with *cement and water*. Specific expressions are used to make this relationship clear like *compared to* and *similar to*. The analogy even extends to the strength of the material: *peanut brittle gets pretty hard, but concrete is even harder.*

If an analogy does not readily come to mind, you should try to include examples that help to make your term more relevant to your audience. If the peanut brittle analogy were not used in this response, there are other examples that could have been shared instead. It is possible to give examples of how the strength of concrete is put to use, as shown in the alternative response that follows.

The last two sentences bring closure to the response and keep it cohesive. First of all the conclusion emphasizes that concrete is *hard* and second that concrete is an *excellent material for construction*. This response follows the five-step strategy for defining concepts or terms presented earlier. This is a solid strategy for communicating the definition and explanation of a concept or term. If you use this strategy well you communicate a sense of fluency, knowledge, and confidence to the rater.

Here is an alternative response that focuses on examples rather than on an analogy.

When we walk through the engineering lab, you'll have a chance to see some of the student projects involving concrete. While you all may know what concrete looks like, you may not know what it's made of. Concrete has three basic components, aggregate, cement, and water. Aggregate includes gravel and sand. Cement acts as a glue. Water is necessary to start the binding action of the cement. Concrete has many uses in society. Concrete foundations hold the weight of large buildings. Concrete runways endure the repeated landings of jumbo jets. Concrete dams hold back tons of water. Concrete can also make our lives more pleasant in smaller ways, like concrete sidewalks for our neighborhoods and concrete benches for our parks. Anyway, concrete is not something that's taken for granted by our engineering faculty and students.

---

⑤ Exercise 19.1: Generating Examples

Now let's work on quickly thinking of examples, because specific examples can be an effective method for communicating ideas. For each of the following categories, list two or three examples. Make sure your examples are specific and relevant to the topic.

1. How to lose weight.

   _____

   _____

   _____

2. The benefits of having someone else proofread a paper you write.

   _____

   _____

   _____

3. The costs and benefits of a state lottery.

   _____

   _____

   _____

4. The importance of voting in a democracy.

   _____

   _____

   _____

5. Surfing the Internet.

   _____

   _____

   _____

Now choose one of the topics—losing weight, proofreading, lottery, democracy, or Internet—and give an oral definition of it, including the details you have listed.

Define or Explain Practice Questions

These practice questions will help you prepare to think quickly and respond concisely to the *define or explain* questions found in the graph section. Work on one practice question at a time. If you preview all the questions at once, you will ruin the spontaneity. Make your practice as realistic as possible by not looking ahead at other questions and by keeping the time limit. For each practice question, record your response. As you listen to your recorded responses, see if you have accurately responded to the specific language function, and if you have appropriately addressed the intended audience. Correct and repeat responses that need improvement.

Practice Question 19.1

Although we are friends, we are interested in different career areas. Think about a typical job position in your field and tell me about the responsibilities of someone with this position. (60 seconds)

Practice Question 19.2

Imagine that I am a friend who is not familiar with the equipment used in your profession. Think about one tool, piece of equipment, or machinery used frequently in your field and tell me how it is used. (60 seconds)

Practice Question 19.3

Imagine that I am a student in your class. Define for me what you mean by plagiarism. (60 seconds)

Practice Question 19.4

Imagine that I'm a friend who is not familiar with your field of study. Please define for me research that is considered excellent in your field. (60 seconds)

Practice Question 19.5

Imagine that you are at a party where no one else attending the party has been to your country. Your friends at the party are interested in the government of your country. Choose one branch or division of government of your country and define it for your friends. (60 seconds)

–20–

Announcement Questions for the SPEAK® Test

In this chapter you will:

- Become familiar with the instructions for the SPEAK® (the TSE® prior to 2004) *announcement* question
- See examples of *announcement* questions and corresponding responses.
- Learn what makes an effective response to *announcement* questions.
- Practice responding to a variety of *announcement* questions.

This is the final question of the exam. You are asked to role-play the part of someone giving an announcement. The announcement will usually have some changes marked on it, and these are the details you should highlight in your announcement. Also think about the intended audience and the best way to address this specific group.

The *announcement* question may be something like this:

> Let's pretend that you are the president of the Glenview Historical Society. Following is an agenda for a trip to Springfield, Illinois. As president of the Glenview Historical Society you have had the responsibility for planning

this trip. You mailed a copy of the trip agenda to all the members of the Glenview Historical Society two weeks ago. Since then, there have been some last-minute changes. Pretend you are at the monthly meeting of the Glenview Historical Society and you want to review the schedule of the trip with the other members and emphasize the changes in the agenda. Because this is an oral presentation to the members of your organization, you do not want to just read the information printed on the agenda. Take the next 60 seconds to plan your presentation. After that you will hear the test narrator ask you to begin your presentation. (90 seconds)

GLENVIEW HISTORICAL SOCIETY
Springfield Trip

Date:	**Friday** ~~Thursday~~, October 13	
Transportation:	Glenview Club Van	
Departure:	**7:30** ~~8:00~~ A.M.	Jefferson Community College
Agenda:	10:00 A.M.	Guided tour of Lincoln's home
	12:00 P.M.	Memorial Carillon (special demonstration)
	12:30 P.M.	Lunch at Washington Park Botanical Gardens*
	2:00 P.M.	The Lincoln Tomb, Oakridge Cemetery
	3:00 P.M.	Illinois State ~~Museum~~ **Capitol**
Return:	5:00 P.M.	
Cost:	**3.00** ~~$5.00~~ per person (to help cover gas)	

---

*Bring your own lunch; drinks available for purchase at the park.

Announcement 1

In responding to this type of question it is important to role-play the part. That is, imagine that you really are the president of the organization and that you really are talking to the members. It will be important to choose language that is appropriate for your audience and for the task of expressing the details of the schedule and highlighting the scheduling changes. Reading the information off the schedule word for word, or without organizational markers or transitions, will make the announcement sound like a telegram and it will not be scored well.

You are given 60 seconds to review the schedule before you need to start speaking. Since you have been asked not to read the information, think of language you can use to package the information in a way that is appropriate to the context. Practice pronouncing words you think you may have trouble saying clearly. For example, if you have trouble pronouncing /th/ or /r/, then consciously practice pronouncing *Thursday* and *thirteen*. Additionally, prepare an opening statement to greet the audience and tell them what you will be talking about. As you look over the details of the schedule, think of ways you can highlight the changes. Also think of a way to bring your presentation to a close. Here is an example response:

> *Good afternoon, ladies and gentlemen of the Glenview His-torical Society. You are all invited on our trip to Springfield. Let's take a few minutes to review the schedule together.*
> *Our trip will take place on Friday, October 13th, not Thursday as was misprinted in the schedule. We will be taking the van, which is very comfortable, and will be leaving from Jefferson Community College at 7:30 A.M. Don't come at 8:00 as originally scheduled or you will miss the van!*
> *Four activities are planned for our time in Springfield. At 10:00 A.M. we will start with a tour of Lincoln's home. From there we will drive to Memorial Carillon for a special noontime demonstration of the bells. This will be followed by lunch at 12:30 P.M. at the Washington Park Botanical Gardens. You should plan on bringing your own lunch, although drinks can be purchased there. At 2:00 P.M. our site-seeing continues at the Lincoln Tomb.*

> *Because the Illinois State Museum is closed this week for repairs, we will be touring the Illinois State Capital instead. Our van will be leaving from the Capital at approximately 5:00 P.M.*
>
> *The cost of the trip is $3, not $5 as originally estimated. If you haven't signed up already, be sure to sign up today before you leave!*

This response begins with a formal greeting from the president of a society to its members, *Good afternoon, ladies and gentlemen.* A teaching assistant addressing a class, or a student addressing other students who are part of a campus club, would probably start out with a less formal greeting like *Hello, everyone.* However, a professor presenting a paper at a conference or an executive giving a report to the board of directors would probably use a formal greeting. Therefore, it is important that you know what role you are supposed to be playing and what audience you are supposed to be talking to in order to appropriately address the audience.

The greeting is followed by a preview of what is to be shared in the announcement. The topic of the trip is introduced with an invitation: *You are all invited.* Then the preview specifically states, *Let's take a few minutes to review the schedule together.* This type of preview tells the audience and the rater what to listen for in the next few minutes. Because the rater has clues on how to listen, the communication becomes more effective.

Public speakers as well as teachers often use inclusive language in order to show unity with the group they are speaking to. Therefore, rather than saying *I will tell you,* the phrase *Let's take a few minutes* was used. Identifying the trip as *our trip* rather than *the trip* and stating that *We will be taking the van,* rather than *the van will be leaving,* makes the announcement sound more inclusive as well. Expressions like *our time in Springfield, we will start with, our site-seeing continues, we will be touring,* and *our van will be leaving* all add to the inclusiveness of the announcement which is the type of atmosphere a president would want to create in an organization.

⑨ Exercise 20.1: Pronouncing Dates

Dates, places, and times should be accurately stated to avoid confusion. Except for the first, second, and third, dates carry a voiceless /th/ sound as in April twelfth. *Most announcements include some kind of dates. Before you take the test, practice pronouncing the 12 months of the year along with various dates such as:*

January first	*February twelfth*	*March thirteenth*
April fourteenth	*May fifteenth*	*June sixteenth*
July seventeenth	*August eighteenth*	*September nineteenth*
October twenty-fifth	*November thirtieth*	*December thirty-first*

Key words to check pronunciation on during the 60 seconds given to prepare your announcement should include all multisyllable place names and nouns. In this example that would include the *Glenview Historical Society; Springfield, Illinois; Jefferson Community College; Memorial Carillon; Washington Park Botanical Gardens; Lincoln Tomb; Oak Ridge Cemetery; the Illinois State Museum;* and *the Illinois State Capital.*

Times can be clearly stated by referring to either A.M. or P.M. In this response, the first morning time was given as 7:30 A.M. When 8:00 was mentioned right after this, no A.M. was used since the time frame had already been established as morning. Clear communication of dates, places, and times allows the rater to accurately follow your announcement.

The schedule of the trip is given in a logical order starting with the date and the departure time and going through each of the activities in order. This is the way the information was given on the written announcement. By talking about the details of the schedule in this order, it makes it easier for the raters to follow your announcement as they follow along on their own copy of the schedule.

Since the schedule will probably have some changes marked on it, you will need to think of wording that can highlight these changes. To make changes clear, the new information is given along with the old information so the audience doesn't just assume what was announced refers to the old information. For example, if all that was announced was Friday October 13th, then a listener might not realize that the 13th was a Friday not a

Thursday. This type of confusion is avoided in the response with the phrase *Friday, October 13th, not Thursday as was misprinted in the schedule.* This contrast of old and new information should further be highlighted by placing primary stress on *Friday* and *Thursday.* The change in plans for the departure time is highlighted in a similar way: *Don't come at 8:00 as originally scheduled or you will miss the van!* The cost of the trip was also changed and the change pointed out: *The cost of the trip is $3 not $5 as originally estimated.* To highlight this contrast, primary stress should be placed on *$3* and *$5.* (For more practice with primary stress on contrasts see Hahn and Dickerson 1998.)

When announcements contain both the old information and new information, it is important to clearly state which is right and which is wrong. Clear statements are made in this response about what is incorrect information, *not Thursday as was misprinted, Don't come, touring the Illinois State Capital instead,* and *not $5.* Clear distinctions between old information and correct information will help to increase your communicative competence rating.

Often there will be an asterisk within the schedule that refers to a footnote at the bottom of the page. Include the footnoted information where appropriate and use complete sentences to explain the footnote. Choose language that relates the information in the footnote to the context of the announcement. Don't just tack on the footnote as an incomplete phrase at the end of your announcement.

As the person giving the announcement, you want to arouse the audience's interest in the information by making it interesting and relevant to them. However, there is not a lot of time to say much beyond what is in the written announcement. Adjectives can be used to create this effect such as *. . . the van, which is very comfortable,* and *. . . special noontime demonstration.* However, be careful not to get sidetracked from the basic announcement. Notice how this response does not try to capture the interest of the audience by discussing the beauty of Washington Park or the details of the Memorial Carillon demonstration. If you try to make the announcement more interesting by trying to share a lot of details that are not in the written announcement, then you will not have time to fully explain the changes in the announcement as the question asks. This will leave the rater with the sense that the stated goal of telling the basic announcement and indicating the changes has not been accomplished.

Transitions and markers help to make your response more cohesive. In this response the phrase *Four activities* clearly marks the transition from departure time to what is planned for the day. The rater is also clued in to specifically listen for four activities. Transitions like, *From there we will drive*, *This will be followed by*, and *our site-seeing continues* indicate a shift from one activity to the next. By using cohesive devices in your response, you demonstrate fluency and control of language to the rater.

The announcement ends with a concluding statement that encourages the audience to participate in this upcoming event. *If you haven't signed up already, be sure to sign up today before you leave!* Encouraging participation demonstrates audience awareness.

An alternative approach to responding to this question would be to refer the audience to the printed schedule and focus on the changes as shown next.

Good afternoon, ladies and gentlemen of the Glenview Historical Society. You are all invited on our trip to Springfield. Please pull out your copies of the schedule so we can briefly review it together. There are four important changes that we all should be aware of.

First of all our trip will take place on Friday, October 13th, not Thursday as was misprinted in the schedule. Please note that on your schedule.

Second, we will be taking the van from Jefferson Community College at 7:30 A.M., not 8:00 A.M. as printed. So don't come at 8:00 or you will miss the van!

We have a full agenda of activities scheduled from 10 A.M. to 5 P.M. Please refer to your schedule for the details. I think you will particularly enjoy the noon demonstration at the Memorial Carillon.

The third change you should mark down is that we will be touring the Illinois State Capital instead of the Illinois State Museum. The State Museum will be closed for repairs; however, I know you will enjoy the Capital.

Finally, and best of all, is that the cost of the trip has been reduced from $5.00 to $3.00. Sign up today before you leave, if you haven't already done so.

A number of useful expressions for highlighting changes are summarized below.

instead
unfortunately
adjusted from _____ to _____
please note that
please make a note of it
we changed
you should be aware
it was necessary to change
originally, . . . but now . . .

⑤ Exercise 20.2: Expressing a Change

In this exercise you are given sets of words, the first is the original information, the second is the change. Think of three ways to express each change. Write out these changes in complete sentences and then say them aloud. The first one has been done for you.

1. leave 9:00 A.M./8:30 A.M.

   • <u>We will be leaving at 8:30 A.M., not 9:00 A.M. as originally scheduled.</u>

   • <u>Please make a note of the change in departure time. We will be leaving at 8:30 A.M., not 9:00.</u>

   • <u>In order to beat the traffic we will be leaving at 8:30 A.M. instead of 9:00.</u>

2. take the bus/car pool

_____

_____

_____

3. date: Thursday, May 17/Friday, May 18

_____

_____

_____

4. lunch at Allan's Steak house/the Vegetarian Cuisine

_____

_____

_____

5. entrance fee $20/$25

_____

_____

_____

Announcement Practice Questions

These practice questions will help you prepare to think quickly and respond concisely to *announcement* questions. Work on one question at a time. If you preview all the questions at once, you will ruin the spontaneity. Make your practice as realistic as possible by not looking ahead at other questions and by keeping the time limit. For each question, record your response. As you listen to your recorded responses, see if you have clearly highlighted the changes in the announcements, and if you have appropriately addressed the intended audience. Correct and repeat responses that need improvement.

Practice Question 20.1

Let's pretend that you are the chairperson of the Greenville Botanical Society. Below you will see an agenda for an upcoming trip to the Botanical Gardens. As chairperson of the Greenville Botanical Society you have had the responsibility for planning this trip. You mailed a copy of the trip agenda to all the Greenville Botanical Society members four weeks ago. Since then, there have been some last-minute changes. Pretend you are at the monthly meeting of the Greenville Botanical Society and you want to review the schedule of the trip with the other members and emphasize the changes in the agenda. Because this is an oral presentation to the members of your organization, you do not want to just read the information printed on the agenda. Take the next 60 seconds to plan your presentation, and then begin your presentation. (90 seconds)

GREENVILLE BOTANICAL SOCIETY

Botanical Gardens Trip

Date:	Saturday, August ~~23~~ 24	
Transportation:	Tourlines Bus Service	
Departure:	~~11:00~~ 10:45 A.M.	Park District Parking Lot B
Agenda:	12:00 P.M.	Lunch at the Garden Cafe
	1:30 P.M.	Tour Wildflower Gardens
	2:30 P.M.	Fields Auditorium
		Special Lecture on ~~Japanese Gardens~~ Flower Arranging
	3:30 P.M.	Guided Tour of Japanese Gardens
	4:15 P.M.	Guilford Tea Room
		Japanese Tea Ceremony*
Return:	5:30 P.M.	
Cost:	~~$12.00~~ $15.00 per person (includes lunch and transportation)	

*No photographing permitted.

Announcement 2

Practice Question 20.2

Let's pretend that you are the social director for the Cosmopolitan Club. Following is an agenda for the 4th of July holiday. As social director of the Cosmopolitan Club you have had the responsibility of planning for this holiday. You just finished passing out a copy of this announcement to all the Cosmopolitan Club members at one of the regular meetings. Since this announcement was printed, there have been some changes. Pretend you need to review the schedule with the other members and emphasize the changes in the agenda. Because this is an oral presentation to the members of your organization you do not want to just read the information printed on the agenda. Take the next 60 seconds to plan your presentation and then begin your presentation. (90 seconds)

COSMOPOLITAN CLUB
July 4th Picnic

Date:	Tuesday, July 4th	
Parade:	1:00 P.M.	Main Street, ~~east side of Pine Grove~~ *between 3rd and 5th Street*
Barbecue:	3:30 P.M.	~~Pine Grove~~ *Rotary* Picnic Shelter
		Please bring:* A–H Side dish or chips
		I–P Salad
		Q–Z Dessert
Games:	~~5:00~~ *4:30* P.M.	Horseshoe contest
	5:30 P.M.	~~Volleyball Match~~ *Softball game*
	6:00 P.M.	3-legged race, all age groups
Fireworks:	8:30 P.M. (or after dusk)	
		Norton Golf Course, north of Pine Grove

---

*Drinks, hamburgers, and table service provided.

Announcement 3

Practice Question 20.3

Let's pretend that you are the president of the University Alumni Association. Following you will see an agenda for an upcoming trip to the University campus. As president of the University Alumni Association you have had the responsibility for planning this trip. You mailed a copy of the trip agenda to all the University Alumni members three weeks ago. Since then, there have been some last-minute changes. Pretend you are at the monthly meeting of the University Alumni Association and you want to review the schedule of the trip with the other members and emphasize the changes in the agenda. Because this is an oral presentation to the members of your organization you do not want to just read the information printed on the agenda. Take the next 60 seconds to plan your presentation, and then begin your presentation. (90 seconds)

UNIVERSITY ALUMNI ASSOCIATION

Campus Visit

Date:		Saturday, October ~~8~~ **12**
Breakfast:	8:15 A.M.	Breakfast at ~~University~~ **Roosevelt** Inn
		Speaker: Prof. Atkins, Biological Sciences
Facilities Tour:	10:00 A.M.	William Hall Research Center
		Tour guide: ~~Prof. Marsh~~ **Prof. Stevenson**, Computer Science
Lunch/Shopping:	~~11:30 A.M.~~ **12:00 P.M.**	Campus Town*
Concert:	3:30 P.M.	Smith Center for the Performing Arts
		Concert Band led by Prof. Rogers, Music
Dinner:	6:30 P.M.	Grand Ballroom, Student Union
		Dancing starting at 8:30 P.M.

---

*Lunch on your own.

Announcement 4

Practice Question 20.4

Let's pretend that you are the instructor for a Chemistry class. Following you will see a schedule for December, the last month of the fall semester. As the instructor for the class you have had the responsibility for planning the syllabus. You just finished passing out a copy of the schedule to all the students in your class. Since the time you photocopied this schedule, you noticed some errors and some last-minute changes. Pretend it is the beginning of class and you want to review the schedule of the trip with your students and emphasize the corrections in the schedule. Because this is an oral presentation to the students in your class, you do not want to just read the information printed on the schedule. Take the next 60 seconds to plan your presentation, and then begin your presentation. (90 seconds)

Chemistry 201

December Schedule

leave campus at 1:30 p.m.

Field Trip:	Friday, December 3
	Plymouth Pharmaceutical Labs
Lab Report 5:	Due Friday, December ~~9~~ *10*
Midterm Exam:*	10:00 A.M., Monday, December 13
	open book, open notes
Final Review Session:	6:30 P.M., Wednesday, December 15
	212 ~~205~~ Chemistry Annex Building
Final Exam:*	*1:00* ~~1:30~~ P.M., Saturday, December 18
	Van Huis Auditorium

---

*Programmable calculators not allowed.

Announcement 5

Practice Question 20.5

Let's pretend that you are the instructor for an Art class. Following you will see a schedule for a field trip to the Art Museum. As the instructor for the class you have had the responsibility for planning this field trip. You handed out a copy of the agenda to all your students at the last class meeting. Since then, you noticed some errors and some last-minute changes. Pretend it is the beginning of the next class and you want to review the agenda of the trip with your students and emphasize the corrections in the schedule. Because this is an oral presentation to the students in your class, you do not want to just read the information printed on the schedule. Take the next 60 seconds to plan your presentation, and then begin your presentation. (90 seconds)

ART 211

Museum Visit

April 4

Date:	Saturday, ~~March 27~~	
Departure:	9:30 A.M.	Bus leaves from the ~~north~~ *west* entrance of the Art & Design Building
Agenda:	11:00 A.M.	Guided tour of ~~European~~ *American* Exhibit
	12:30 P.M.	Lunch at the Watercolor Cafe*
	1:30 P.M.	Watkins Auditorium special lecture on Modern Art by ~~Harriett Shields, Director~~ *Debbie Farrell, Assist Dir.*
	2:30 P.M.	Guided tour of Egyptian Art Exhibit
	3:30 P.M.	Free time to view exhibits
Return:	*5:30* ~~5:00~~ P.M.	Bus leaves from the main entrance to the Art Museum

*Bring money for lunch.

Announcement 6

Answers Key for Selected Exercises

Exercise 3.3 (page 32)

1. L, 2. L, 3. L, 4. RM, 5. L, 6. RM, 7. RM, 8. RM, 9. L, 10. H, 11. H, 12. L, 13. RM

Exercise 7.1 (page 84)

Paragraph 1: (a) 11, (b) 4, (c) 5, (d) 6, (e) 1, (f) 10, (g) 7, (h) 2, (i) 12, (j) 9, (k) 8, (l) 3

Paragraph 2: (a) 11, (b) 6, (c) 1, (d) 5, (e) 8, (f) 9, (g) 2, (h) 7, (i) 10, (j) 3, (k) 4

Exercise 11.3 (page 147)
Answers may vary but could include the following:

2. more students coming

3. apply to the university

4. student applications are growing

5. so the number of students that could be admitted is also increasing

6. there is a temporary decline

Exercise 12.1 (page 163)

Response A: 1. RM, 2. L, 3. L , 4. L, 5. L, 6. L, 7. L, 8. RM, 9. L, 10. L

Response B: 1. RM, 2. L, 3. L, 4. RM, 5. L, 6. RM, 7. L, 8. RM, 9. RM, 10. L

Bibliography

Celce-Murcia, M., and D. Larsen-Freeman. *The Grammar Book: An ESL/EFL Teacher's Course.* Rowley, MA: Newbury House Publisher, Inc., 1983.

Division of Measurement and Evaluation, University of Illinois. *Q & A* 2, no. 1 (Fall 1994).

———. *Q & A* 2, no. 2 (1995).

Educational Testing Service. *TSE Score User's Manual.* Princeton, NJ: ETS, 1995.

———. *SPEAK Rater Training Guide.* Princeton, NJ: ETS, 1996.

———. *TSE Bulletin 2003–4,* Princeton, NJ: ETS, 2003.

Hahn, L., and W. Dickerson. *Speechcraft: Discourse Pronunciation for Advanced Learners.* Ann Arbor: University of Michigan Press, 1998.

Hopkins, K. D., J. C. Stanley, and B. R. Hopkins. *Educational and Psychological Measurement and Evaluation.* Englewood Cliffs, NJ: Prentice-Hall, 1990.

Papajohn, D. "Test Preparation: Misconceptions and Realities." *TESOL Matters* 10, no. 4 (2002).

Sarwark, S. M., J. Smith, R. MacCallum, and E. C. Cascallar. *A Study of Characteristics of the SPEAK Test.* ETS Research Report 49. Princeton, NJ: ETS, 1995.

Smith, J., C. M. Meyers, and A. J. Burkhalter. *Communicate: Strategies for International Teaching Assistants.* Englewood Cliffs, NJ: Regents/Prentice-Hall, 1992.

Wennerstrom, A. *Techniques for Teachers: A Guide for Nonnative Speakers of English.* Ann Arbor: University of Michigan Press, 1991.